W9-DGG-633

THE WORKS AND DAYS

THEOGONY

THE SHIELD OF HERAKLES

*the Works
and Days*

Theogony

*the Shield
of Herakles*

HESIOD

translated by Richmond Lattimore

illustrated by Richard Wilt

ANN ARBOR PAPERBACKS

THE UNIVERSITY OF MICHIGAN PRESS

First edition as an Ann Arbor Paperback 1991
Designed by George Lenox
Copyright © by the University of Michigan 1959,
renewed 1987 by Alice Lattimore
All rights reserved
ISBN 0-472-43903-0 (clothbound)
ISBN 0-472-08161-6 (paperbound)
Library of Congress Catalog Card No. 59-6072

Published in the United States of America by
The University of Michigan Press
Manufactured in the United States of America

2002   *29   28*

A CIP catalogue record for this book is available
from the British Library.

No part of this publication may be reproduced, stored in
a retrieval system, or transmitted in any form or by any
means, electronic, mechanical, or otherwise without the
written permission of the publisher.

Contents

Introduction

The purpose of Homeric epic is principally to tell stories. Its materials are drawn from a series of events which took place, or are imagined to have taken place, not later than the twelfth century B.C. In the final form in which we find the two great Homeric poems, composed probably late in the eighth century B.C.,* these events have been shaped and centered about the story of Troy, and emphasize in particular the actions of certain great heroes at the siege, and the further adventures and homecoming of one particular hero. The gaps in the whole saga were then filled in by the successors of Homer (in the now lost "Epic Cycle") until there was a complete narrative, in hexameter verse, which told the story of Troy from beginning to end. The aim of these successors was, to judge by fragments and summaries of them, even more exclusively narrative than was Homer's.

Materially, then, the Homeric epic tells the stories of the heroic age, some four centuries at least after the events themselves, and when the poet strays into his own present, this is accidental and incidental. Formally,

* I follow generally the "late" chronology, which will be conveniently found in, for instance, Bury's *History of Greece* (third edition, with the essential revisions of Russell Meiggs, London: Macmillan, 1955).

the Homeric epic is composed in regular hexameter verse, and abounds in formulaic lines and metrical units. Since it is impossible that the meter itself, its formulae, and the material all originated with the final author (or authors) of the *Iliad* and *Odyssey*, we are forced to infer a long period of growth and crystallization of saga and metrical expressions alike, which involved generations of storytelling poets, now nameless and lost, between the events themselves and the completion of the two great Homeric poems.

We do not know where these poets, or Homer himself, lived. The successors of Homer came from various parts of Greece, on both sides of the Aegean. Homer himself is generally placed in the central part of Greek Asia Minor, in the region of Smyrna and Chios. The works of Homer, his predecessors, and his successors are often handily lumped together under the term "Ionian epic."

In Boiotia, in central Greece, there was an epic tradition which seems to have been at least partly independent. It produced three major works: the *Theogony*; the *Catalogue of Women* or *Eoiai* (preserved only in fragments, but to which is attached, as an excursus, *The Shield of Herakles*); and *The Works and Days*; and numerous minor, or worse attested, poems.*

Let us for the moment leave in abeyance the question of Hesiodic authorship and speak simply of

---

* Titles and fragments are to be found in Evelyn-White's Loeb edition (see bibliography). They include *The Divination by Birds, The Astronomy, The Precepts of Chiron, The Idaian Dactyls, The Marriage of Keÿx, The Melampodia, The Aigimios, The Great Works, The Great Eoiai,* and *Theseus and Peirithoös.* The relation of *The Great Works* to *The Works and Days* has been hitherto quite obscure, as is that of *The Great Eoiai* to *The Eoiai.*

Boiotian epic. This is composed in the same meter and virtually the same dialect as Homeric epic. It uses formulae which occur in Homeric epic but generates other formulae of its own. The identity of the major gods and heroes agrees in the main with the Homeric.

Boiotian epic, in contrast to the work of the successors of Homer, does not concern itself mainly in filling out the narrative of the Trojan saga. In fact, the poets of the Boiotian epic are not principally storytellers. Yet extended poetry must have some containing frame. Boiotia favors the catalogue and the genealogy: who is who, and what is what, and how they came to be; and again, the moral: these things being so, why; and what to do. Such elements, fundamental to Boiotian, are incidental to Homeric epic; when they do become primary in Homer, as in the *Iliad*'s "Catalogue of Ships" (which opens with Boiotia) or the *Odyssey*'s "Procession of Heroines," it has always been felt that Boiotia has crept in. And so it has, but this does not have to indicate some late mean interpolator ramming his dull stuff into a lively finished work. It may just as well mean interchange between two collateral living traditions which, while separate, are by no means mutually ignorant.

Homer did not invent the whole style and substance of his final poems. There were Homeric poets, generations of them, before Homer. It is reasonable, at least, to guess that there were Boiotian or "Hesiodic" poets before Hesiod, that he, like Homer, inherited and perfected a tradition, rather than merely importing his version of Homer into Boiotia. If he had predecessors, we do not know their names, but neither do we know the names of Homer's predecessors. Before we consider, therefore, the authorship of the three major Boiotian poems, we should be aware that Hesiod, rather than founding a school, might have come relatively late into a living tradition.

HESIOD

Most of what we know about Hesiod comes from certain apparently unpremeditated asides in *The Works and Days*. Hesiod's father was a merchant who found the going hard and came from Kyme in Aiolia (Greek Asia Minor) to Askra, in the territory of Thespiai, and settled there as a farmer (*Works and Days* 633–40). There he died and left his property to be divided between his two sons, Hesiod and Perses. Hesiod accuses Perses of seizing the better share by bribing the "kings," who seem to be barons, country squires, or justices of the peace (*Works and Days* 27–39). *The Works and Days* has as its guiding thread the outline of a useful farmer's life addressed to this scapegrace Perses, although the theme produces often a more general address and expression. Often it suggests itself as the single work, evoked by a particular occasion, of an amateur poet who was really a farmer. But this was not exactly the case. Hesiod had already been to Euboia to compete, with a poem, at the funeral games of Amphidamas (*Works and Days* 651–59) and had won a prize. The proem to the *Theogony*, especially lines 22–35, not only makes it clear that Hesiod wrote this poem also * but strongly suggests that poetry was his chief business. We can, perhaps, infer a little more about him from the poems. He spoke for the people, but was not of the poorest class. *The Works and Days* is addressed to a freeholder who "routs out his people," that is, has others working for him, though he does

---

* Deliberate forgery is, of course, possible. It always is.

manual work himself too. Hesiod had scarcely traveled at all when he wrote *The Works and Days*. Nothing in his manner or matter ever suggests that he had seen war at first hand. Family? Wife? Children? *The Works and Days* rather suggests a bachelor, but a susceptible one.

As to this, finally, there is the story of Hesiod's death, contained in the *vita* attached to the manuscripts, and elsewhere. He is supposed to have been warned by the Delphic oracle to avoid the grove of Nemean Zeus, but believing this meant the famous Nemea in the Peloponnese, he failed to note that Oinoë in Lokris was also sacred to Nemean Zeus. He visited there, seduced the sister of his hosts, they murdered him and threw him into the sea, but dolphins brought the body ashore. The child of the affair was the Lokrian lyric poet, Stesichorus. It is true that there was a sanctuary of Nemean Zeus at Lokrian Oinoë, as Thucydides (3. 96. 1) attests, and Thucydides knew the story as one "told by the local people." But the story is probably a fiction, or if it contains some germ of truth, this is so overgrown with folklore motives as to be inextricable.

a. Stesichorus seems pretty firmly established in mid-sixth-century, and not even the most resolute late-dater would dare bring Hesiod down far enough to make him the father. Stesichorus is "the son of Hesiod" because he drew heavily on the Hesiodic poems, particularly the *Catalogue*.

b. The ambiguous and misunderstood oracle of this sort is a folk-motive that works into the History of Herodotus (3. 64. 3–5; 9. 33) as well as the biography of Euripides and elsewhere. There can, of course, be genuine reports of responses given, and this could be one.

c. Ancient biographical tradition liked things lurid, and was not disposed to let great men die tamely in bed. Deaths gruesome or quaint or melodramatic are reported, in one place or another, for Aeschylus, Sophocles, Euripides, Heracleitus, Empedocles, Ibycus, Terpander, Sappho, and Anacreon.

It may be unscientific to damn for guilt by association. In this case, I find the combination too rich to be persuasive. But part of the story may be true.

THE HESIODIC POEMS

The Works and Days. Here it is worth while to quote Pausanias, the traveler (second century A.D.; Pausanias 9. 31. 4–5, Frazer's translation):

The Boeotians of Helicon have a tradition that Hesiod composed nothing but the *Works*, and even from it they strike out the preliminary address to the Muses, saying that the poem begins with the passage about the Strifes. They showed me also beside the spring a leaden tablet, very time-worn, on which are engraved the *Works*. There is another opinion, quite distinct from the former, that Hesiod composed a great number of poems, namely, the poem on women, the poem called the *Great Eoeae,* the *Theogony,* the poem on the soothsayer Melampus, the poem on the descent of Theseus and Pirithous to hell, the *Precepts of Chiron for the Instruction of Achilles,* and various other poems besides the *Works and Days.* Those who hold this view also say that Hesiod was taught soothsaying by the Acarnanians, and there is a poem on soothsaying, which I have myself read, and a work on the interpretation of prodigies.

Rather than give a separate outline of the structure of this poem, I have appended a running analysis to the translated text, in the hope that this might be more illuminating. The keys to the construction of *The Works and Days* lie, I think, not in any scheme we can recover, but in the transitions of thought.

The *Theogony*. Despite the remarks of Pausanias quoted above, this ought to be regarded as the work of Hesiod. It is "signed," so to speak. Deliberate forgery is possible, but unlikely. The purpose is, in the Boiotian manner, descriptive, or better expository, rather than narrative. We reach what was from the consideration of what is. The narrative of the battle between Olympians and Titans (629–735), with the epic discourse that goes with epic combat, is the most forcedly artificial part of the poem. That is, of course, only my opinion; but it is fact that the whole passage enters as an afterthought hung on a *gar* clause.

There is much material in the *Theogony* which is not in Homer, but the two poets agree almost invariably on the identities of the gods, differences being in matters of emphasis. As Herodotus says (2. 53. 2): "I think Homer and Hesiod date to four hundred years before my time, and not more. These are the ones who made the *Theogony* (or established the generation of the gods) for the Hellenes, assigned them their supplementary names and relative positions, explained their special functions, and described their appearances." The statement fits Hesiod better than Homer, but Homer agrees with Hesiod, or follows, if not Hesiod, then Hesiod's ultimate sources. Hesiod himself did not name the gods—he catalogued them; by means, chiefly, of genealogical classification. He is, in a way, the first Greek theologian, and so, in a vaguer way, the first philosopher. Homer's gods serve narrative; narrative for human beings must use human characters, however eagerly disguised; so Homer's gods are really people, and Homer is basically antitheologi-

cal and antiphilosophical. This was constantly acknowl-
edged by Socrates and Plato.

The authority of Hesiod's arrangement went largely
unchallenged. But though most Greeks believed, and
many modern scholars believe, that the *Theogony* is
Hesiod's, the very method of it, by entry and expansion,
permits and positively invites interpolation or further
expansion. Not only could this happen, it has hap-
pened. Our present text contains two different versions
of the story of Zeus and Metis (ll. 886–900; 929e–t,
see Evelyn-White, *op. cit.*). At 904–6 Klotho, Lachesis,
and Atropos are made daughters of Zeus and Themis;
this contradicts not only most Greek tradition but
lines 217–18, where they are daughters of Night. It is
possible that a genuine *Theogony* of Hesiod was
known, by people like Plutarch's informants, to have
been so tampered with and "improved" that the honor
of the whole work was compromised.

The *Catalogue* (*of Women*) or *Eoiai*. This was a
work of major interest, importance, and, so far as we
can judge, quality. We have no manuscript, but many
quotations, and since, fortunately, it was known in
Greek Egypt, papyrus fragments have been appearing
and there is hope for better knowledge in the future.*

Our *Theogony* ends with a list of goddesses who
mated with mortals and then, last of all, two lines,
which may of course have been a later joining piece,†
to bring in a catalogue of women. As would be ex-
pected from the arrangement, many of these were
temporary paramours of gods, by whom they generated
the ancestral heroes of the Greek peoples. The formula
ē hoiē, "or like her who . . . ," was so often repeated

* The latest are to be found in *Oxyrhynchus Papyri*, Part 23,
edited by E. Lobel (London: Egypt Exploration Society, 1956).
† But at least early enough to be included in a papyrus of the
2d century A.D. (so dated by Lobel, *op. cit.*, pp. 1–3).

that it produced the title *Eoiai*, which is either an alternative title to the *Catalogue*, or the title of the last part of it, or an addition to it. We can not be sure.

Women predominate not only, I think, because of matriarchal considerations, or claims to divine paternity, but also because Boiotian tradition leans in every way toward the distaff side. Yet, through entry and identification of the heroine "like her who . . . ," one can file the heroes too, and their exploits, and so compose an account of the heroic age using a method different from Homer's and scarcely derived from him. The work did, in fact, incorporate legendary material not only from Boiotia and southern Thessaly but from the whole of mainland Greece. Like the *Theogony*, the *Catalogue*, so composed, permits the building-in of supplementary material without undue strain. We have a case attested, for the Argument to *The Shield of Herakles* states that the first fifty-six lines are from the Fourth Book of the *Catalogue*. To regard the rest of the *Shield* as the work of a later interpolator is, in view of this, a temperate opinion—and very welcome, too, for the poetry of the rest of the *Shield* seems to most, and to me, to be sub-Hesiodic, though it does have its moments.

But whether or not the original *Catalogue* is Hesiod's, it would do him credit, and shows some of his special character. I would illustrate from an extant fragment (actually a combination of two) which may conveniently be found in Evelyn-White's collection, pp. 192–203.

We are in a catalogue of the suitors of Helen (she probably generated the series with *ē hoiē*) interesting in itself and containing the first mention of that subsequently famous oath of the suitors which Homer ignored. Menelaos won her; her child was Hermione.

. . . but all the gods were quarreling, and their purpose
divided, and already Zeus who thunders on high
was planning monstrous events; to blast a confusion of
tempests over the endless earth; for he was now urgent to
obliterate the great race of mankind; and the end in view
was the destruction of the lives of the demigods,
so the children of the gods might no longer mate with
wretched mortals,
and so look forward to doom; so the blessed ones might
hereafter,
as in the past, have their own life, and their own ways,
apart from humanity . . .

In addition to such cataclysms of nature, Zeus
planned a war. Men, and other gods too, failed to see
what he was about. The portents of nature continued.

From tall-towering trees the leaves came tumbling down
in abundance
and piled the ground in their splendor, and the fruit blew
groundward
as Boreas, by consent of Zeus, blew with a hard blast
and the sea boiled, and everything was shaken from his
blowing,
and the strength of men was shriveled away, and the fruit
diminished
in the spring season
                              at the time when old Hairless, the
Snake,
on the mountains, in the caves of the ground, every three
years produces
three young.
                    In summer, on the mountain, in thick growths
and in the bushes,
he lives, skulking off by himself, in hate avoiding the
beaten
tracks of men, away in the mountainous folds and projec-
tions,

but as winter comes on, under the ground in a deep hole
he lies, with a covering of numerous leaves piled on him,
a horrid snake, spangled on the back with his terrible
  markings;
but when he becomes mutinous and violent beyond telling,
the shafts of Zeus bring him down . . .
and only the soul of him is left, under the divine earth,
and about the self-mounded burial chamber it flitters,
  gibbering
a little; and it comes, faint now, to the sacrifices
made on the wide-wayed earth . . .

This fragment, torn and distracted as it is, shows the
very essence and sinew of Hesiodic work. Heroic legend
at the outset leads into myth of cataclysm. The question behind it all seems to be: "Why are things as
they are, not as we imagine they used to be, and why
does God, who should be man's friend, appear as his
enemy?" The myths of change are frequent and
varied: the Pandora story, the Trojan War, the Great
Flood, or such a cataclysm as Aeschylus offers at the
end of *Prometheus Bound*. Nature has changed; what
we have above might well be a description of the very
first autumn coming to man after a life lived always in
springtime or summertime. The transitional generation
of the poem is thoroughly Boiotian. Note how, from
heroine and heroic legend, we come to, and go from,
the snake. Old Hairless enters, like old No-Bones the
polyp, as a marker of time; he holds the stage briefly in
his own character, an actual snake; he leaves like a com-
mentary on those pictures which show the soul-snake,
and the little flittering soul-ideas, at the tomb.

Hesiod, nevertheless, may not have written the *Catalogue*, for he does not have to have been a lonely
phenomenon in Boiotia. Whoever composed it, the
influence of the work was very great. Not only

Stesichorus but also Pindar drew heavily on it, and whether indirectly through Stesichorus, or directly, it strongly affected Aeschylus and the traditions of Attic Tragedy.

DATES

To Herodotus, Homer and Hesiod were contemporaries. Also, ancient tradition made Hesiod's successful competition at Chalkis (*Works and Days* 651–59) into a contest between Homer and Hesiod. Modern opinion tends to put Hesiod later. What seem to be the two main reasons for this are not, I think, entirely sound.

a. It is assumed that, since Hesiod uses the meter, the formulae, and much of the material of Homer, he must be derivative. But this would not follow if there was an authentic collateral Boiotian tradition. I have tried, above, to show that this is not only possible but likely, though I realize that nothing can be proved. I am afraid, too, that Hesiod has been put after Homer and made dependent on him partly through that low opinion of Boiotian culture into which Athenian prejudice has gulled us all.

b. Hesiod reflects a world later than Homer's. Yes, but Homer was deliberately telling about a period long before his own time. Boiotian epic, as I have tried to show, starts from the present.

I believe, nevertheless, that Hesiod is a little later than Homer. The best piece of evidence is precisely the one which has bothered many scholars in the past. Hesiod's competition, mentioned above, was at the funeral games for Amphidamas, who was a figure in the Lelantine War and whose death ought then not to have taken place before the end of the eighth, or the beginning of the seventh, century. This seems about right, but it is a little later than I should care to go for the Homeric poems—at least, for *The Iliad*. I would settle for a Hesiod who was a younger contemporary of Homer, or—if we are to have two Homers—a younger contemporary of the author of *The Odyssey*.

BIBLIOGRAPHY

Burn, A. R., *The World of Hesiod* (London: Kegan Paul Trench Trubner, 1936).

Evelyn-White, H. G., *Hesiod, the Homeric Hymns, and Homerica* (ed. and trans.; 2d ed.; Cambridge, Mass.; Loeb Series, 1936).

Mair, J., *Hesiod* (trans.; Oxford: Oxford University Press, 1908).

Mazon, P., *Hésiode* (ed. and trans.; Paris: Budé Series, 1928).

Rzach, A., *Hesiodi Carmina* (3d ed.; Leipzig: Teubner, 1913).

Schmid, W., *Geschichte der Griechischen Literatur* (Munich: Beck, 1929), Pt. 1, Vol. 1, esp. pp. 246–89.

Sinclair, T. A., *Hesiod, Works and Days* (London: Macmillan, 1932).

Sittl, K., Ἡσιόδου τὰ Ἅπαντα (Athens, 1889).

Solmsen, F., *Hesiod and Aeschylus* (Ithaca, N.Y.: Cornell University Press, 1949).

The text of Evelyn-White, cited above, has been used in making this translation. Line numbers refer to the Greek text, which seems to contain some corrupt lines. These have often been simply deleted, sometimes given with square brackets.

the Works and Days

To the Muses of Pieria:
tell of Zeus your father

To Zeus: hear and direct

To Perses (my brother):
listen to me

There are two ways of trying
to beat others

One means Trouble and Fighting

But the other is only
Healthy Competition

Muses, who from Pieria give glory through singing,
come to me, tell of Zeus, your own father,
  sing his praises, through whose will
mortal men are named in speech or remain unspoken.
Men are renowned or remain unsung
  as great Zeus wills it.
5 For lightly he makes strong,
  and lightly brings strength to confusion,
lightly diminishes the great man,
  uplifts the obscure one,
lightly the crooked man he straightens,
  withers the proud man,
he, Zeus, of the towering thunders,
  whose house is highest.

Hear me, see me, Zeus: hearken:
  direct your decrees in righteousness.
10 To you, Perses, I would describe
  the true way of existence.

It was never true that there was only one kind
  of strife. There have always
been two on earth. There is one
  you could like when you understand her.
The other is hateful. The two Strifes
  have separate natures.
There is one Strife who builds up evil war,
  and slaughter.
15 She is harsh; no man loves her, but under compulsion
and by will of the immortals men
  promote this rough Strife.
But the other one was born
  the elder daughter of black Night.

Stay away from the wrong kind

Mind your own business,
you'll have no time

(until you're supplied for a year)

to go after *others'* goods

The son of Kronos, who sits on high and
  dwells in the bright air,

Kronos = father of the gods

set her in the roots of the earth and among men;
  she is far kinder.

10 She pushes the shiftless man to work,
  for all his laziness.

A man looks at his neighbor, who is rich:
  then he too

wants work; for the rich man presses on with
  his plowing and planting

and the ordering of his state.
  So the neighbor envies the neighbor   *relevant today*

who presses on toward wealth. Such Strife
  is a good friend to mortals.

25 Then potter is potter's enemy, and
  craftsman is craftman's

rival; tramp is jealous of tramp,
  and singer of singer.

      So you, Perses, put all this firmly away
  in your heart,

nor let that Strife who loves mischief
  keep you from working

as you listen at the meeting place
  to see what you can make of

30 the quarrels. The time comes short for litigations
  and lawsuits,

too short, unless there is a year's living
  laid away inside

for you, the stuff that the earth yields,
  the pride of Demeter.

Demeter = mother of Persephone

When you have got a full burden of that,
  you can push your lawsuits,

Do not try to be too clever

as you and your judges did before, with my share

Easier isn't better

There *is* no easy way any more

ever since

Prometheus tried to be too clever
to outwit Zeus,
to make things easy for men

scheming for other men's goods, yet you
shall not be given another chance
35 to do so. No, come, let us finally settle
our quarrel
⌈ with straight decisions, which are from Zeus, ⌉
⌊ and are the fairest. ⌋
Now once before we divided our inheritance,
but you seized
the greater part and made off with it,
gratifying those barons
who eat bribes, who are willing
to give out such a decision.
40 Fools all! who never learned
how much better than the whole the half is,
nor how much good there is
in living on mallow and asphodel.
For the gods have hidden and keep hidden
what could be men's livelihood.
It could have been that easily
in one day you could work out
enough to keep you for a year,
with no more working.
45 Soon you could have hung up your steering oar
in the smoke of the fireplace,
and the work the oxen and patient mules do
would be abolished,
but Zeus in the anger of his heart hid it away
because the devious-minded Prometheus had cheated him;
and therefore Zeus thought up dismal sorrows
for mankind.
50 He hid fire; but Prometheus, the powerful son
of Iapetos,

Zeus punished Prometheus

by stealing fire
which Zeus had hidden

To pay for this, Zeus promised men
an evil thing

So the gods made the evil
in the form of a lovely, living woman

(Who may be called Woman or Eve or Beauty)

She has everything good

except a good heart

stole it again from Zeus of the counsels,
  to give to mortals.
He hid it out of the sight of Zeus
  who delights in thunder
in the hollow fennel stalk. In anger
  the cloud-gatherer spoke to him:
"Son of Iapetos, deviser of crafts beyond all others,
55 you are happy that you stole the fire,
  and outwitted my thinking;
but it will be a great sorrow to you,
  and to men who come after.
As the price of fire I will give them an evil,
  and all men shall fondle
this, their evil, close to their hearts,
  and take delight in it."
  So spoke the father of gods and mortals;
  and laughed out loud.
60 He told glorious Hephaistos to make haste, and plaster
earth with water, and to infuse it with a human voice
and vigor, and make the face
  like the immortal goddesses,
the bewitching features of a young girl;   Athene: war +
  meanwhile Athene   wisdom.
was to teach her her skills, and how
  to do the intricate weaving,
65 while Aphrodite was to mist her head   → Aphrodite:
  in golden endearment   love + beauty
and the cruelty of desire and longings
  that wear out the body,
but to Hermes, the guide, the slayer of Argos,
  he gave instructions   Hermes: messenger
to put in her the mind of a hussy,   of the gods
  and a treacherous nature.

But Zeus called her Pandora

which means she is given everything

Epimetheus (Afterthought)
forgot his brother's warning
and took her

Kronos tried to kill his off- spring

So Zeus spoke. And all obeyed Lord Zeus,
 the son of Kronos.

70 The renowned strong smith modeled her figure of earth,
  in the likeness
of a decorous young girl, as the son of Kronos
  had wished it.
The goddess gray-eyed Athene dressed and arrayed her;
  the Graces,
who are goddesses, and hallowed Persuasion
  put necklaces
of gold upon her body, while the Seasons,
  with glorious tresses,
75 put upon her head a coronal of spring flowers,
 [and Pallas Athene put all decor upon her body].
But into her heart Hermes, the guide,
  the slayer of Argos,
put lies, and wheedling words
  of falsehood, and a treacherous nature,
made her as Zeus of the deep thunder wished,
  and he, the gods' herald,
80 put a voice inside her, and gave her
  the name of woman,
Pandora, because all the gods *Pandora's Box !!*
 who have their homes on Olympos
had given her each a gift, to be a sorrow to men
who eat bread. Now when he had done
  with this sheer, impossible
deception, the Father sent the gods' fleet messenger,
  Hermes,
85 to Epimetheus, bringing her, a gift,
  nor did Epimetheus
remember to think how Prometheus had told him never

and men have been miserable
ever since

She opened the jar and let
sicknesses and troubles fly
about the world

to accept a gift from Olympian Zeus,
 but always to send it
back, for fear it might prove
 to be an evil for mankind.
He took the evil, and only perceived it
 when he possessed her.

90   Since before this time the races of men
 had been living on earth
free from all evils, free from laborious work,
 and free from
all wearing sicknesses that bring
 their fates down on men
[for men grow old suddenly
 in the midst of misfortune];
but the woman, with her hands lifting away the lid
 from the great jar,
95 scattered its contents, and her design
 was sad troubles for mankind.
Hope was the only spirit that stayed there
 in the unbreakable
closure of the jar, under its rim,
 and could not fly forth
abroad, for the lid of the great jar
 closed down first and contained her;
this was by the will of cloud-gathering Zeus
 of the aegis;
100   but there are other troubles by thousands
 that hover about men,
for the earth is full of evil things,
 and the sea is full of them;
there are sicknesses that come to men by day,
 while in the night

[handwritten marginal note: Pandora released evil into the world, only thing that is left is hope.]

The same thing may be said in a
different way, as

that the world has been steadily
getting worse, and that easy
life we want is lost way
back in the beginning

The good Golden Age (whose
people are now beneficent
spirits)

moving of themselves they haunt us,
   bringing sorrow to mortals,
and silently, for Zeus of the counsels
   took the voice out of them.

105   So there is no way to avoid what Zeus has intended.

Or if you will, I will outline it for you
   in a different story,
well and knowledgeably—store it up
   in your understanding—
the beginnings of things, which were the same for gods
   as for mortals.

In the beginning, the immortals
   who have their homes on Olympos
110   created the golden generation of mortal people.
These lived in Kronos' time, when he
   was the king in heaven.
They lived as if they were gods,
   their hearts free from all sorrow,
by themselves, and without hard work or pain;
   no miserable
old age came their way; their hands, their feet,
   did not alter.
115   They took their pleasure in festivals,
   and lived without troubles.
When they died, it was as if they fell asleep.
   All goods
were theirs. The fruitful grainland
   yielded its harvest to them
of its own accord; this was great and abundant,
   while they at their pleasure

[handwritten margin note: immortals lived a good life on Olympus]

Was followed by the silly
Silver Age

quietly looked after their works,
  in the midst of good things
120 [prosperous in flocks, on friendly terms
  with the blessed immortals].

  Now that the earth has gathered over this generation,
these are called pure and blessed spirits;
  they live upon earth,
and are good, they watch over mortal men
  and defend them from evil;
they keep watch over lawsuits and hard dealings;
  they mantle
125 themselves in dark mist
  and wander all over the country;
they bestow wealth; for this right
  as of kings was given them.
  Next after these the dwellers upon Olympos created
a second generation, of silver, far worse
  than the other.
They were not like the golden ones either in shape
  or spirit.
130 A child was a child for a hundred years,
  looked after and playing
by his gracious mother, kept at home,
  a complete booby. ? ? ?
But when it came time for them to grow up
  and gain full measure,
they lived for only a poor short time;
  by their own foolishness
they had troubles, for they were not able
  to keep away from
135 reckless crime against each other,
  nor would they worship

but these men also are now
spirits

Then came the fierce Bronze
People

Who nevertheless were mortal
and died

the gods, nor do sacrifice on the sacred altars
  of the blessed ones,
which is the right thing among the customs of men,
  and therefore
Zeus, son of Kronos, in anger engulfed them,
  for they paid no due
honors to the blessed gods who live on Olympos.

140   But when the earth had gathered over this generation
also—and they too are called blessed spirits
  by men, though under   —> *Underworld, led by*
the ground, and secondary, but still   *Hades*
  they have their due worship—
then Zeus the father created the third generation
  of mortals,
the age of bronze. They were not like
  the generation of silver.
145 They came from ash spears. They were terrible
  and strong, and the ghastly
action of Ares was theirs, and violence.
  They ate no bread,
but maintained an indomitable and adamantine spirit.
None could come near them; their strength was big,
  and from their shoulders
the arms grew irresistible on their ponderous bodies.
150 The weapons of these men were bronze,
  of bronze their houses,
and they worked as bronzesmiths. There was not yet
  any black iron.
Yet even these, destroyed beneath the hands
  of each other,
went down into the moldering domain of cold Hades;
nameless; for all they were formidable black death

followed by the great age of
the Heroes

who perished in such wars as those
at Thebes and Troy

but others went west to the end of
the world

and live there in bliss even
today

155 seized them, and they had to forsake
    the shining sunlight.

Now when the earth had gathered over this generation
also, Zeus, son of Kronos, created yet another
fourth generation on the fertile earth,
    and these were better and nobler,
the wonderful generation of hero-men, who are also
160 called half-gods, the generation before our own
    on this vast earth. *DEMI-GODS like Perseus.*
But of these too, evil war and the terrible carnage *half*
took some; some by seven-gated Thebes *god, half*
    in the land of Kadmos *human*
as they fought together over the flocks of Oidipous;
    others
war had taken in ships over the great gulf
    of the sea,
165 where they also fought for the sake
    of lovely-haired Helen.
There, for these, the end of death was misted
    about them.
But on others Zeus, son of Kronos, settled a living
    and a country
of their own, apart from human kind,
    at the end of the world.
And there they have their dwelling place,
    and hearts free of sorrow
in the islands of the blessed
    by the deep-swirling stream of the ocean,
prospering heroes, on whom in every year
    three times over
the fruitful grainland bestows its sweet yield.
    These live

Then Zeus made the Fifth
Age, of Iron

mine

I wish it were not

Zeus will destroy this age too

When it has gone bad and lost
all sense of right and wrong

far from the immortals, and Kronos
  is king among them.
For Zeus, father of gods and mortals,
  set him free from his bondage,
although the position and the glory still belong
  to the young gods.

After this, Zeus of the wide brows
  established yet one more
generation of men, the fifth, to be
  on the fertile earth.

And I wish that I were not any part
  of the fifth generation   *mortals*.
of men, but had died before it came,
  or been born afterward.
For here now is the age of iron. Never by daytime
will there be an end to hard work and pain,
  nor in the night
to weariness, when the gods will send anxieties
  to trouble us.
Yet here also there shall be some good things
  mixed with the evils.
180 But Zeus will destroy this generation of mortals
  also,
in the time when children, as they are born,
  grow gray on the temples,
when the father no longer agrees with the children,
  nor children with their father,
when guest is no longer at one with host,
  nor companion to companion,
when your brother is no longer your friend,
  as he was in the old days.

and becomes an Age of Force

185 Men will deprive their parents of all rights,
    as they grow old,
and people will mock them too,
    babbling bitter words against them,
harshly, and without shame in the sight of the gods;
    not even
to their aging parents will they give back
    what once was given.
Strong of hand, one man shall seek
    the city of another.
190 There will be no favor for the man
    who keeps his oath, for the righteous
and the good man, rather men shall give their praise
    to violence
and the doer of evil. Right will be in the arm.
    Shame will
not be. The vile man will crowd his better out,
    and attack him
with twisted accusations and swear an oath
    to his story.
195 The spirit of Envy, with grim face
    and screaming voice, who delights

"delights in evil"

in evil, will be the constant companion
    of wretched humanity,
and at last Nemesis and Aidos, Decency and Respect,
    shrouding
their bright forms in pale mantles, shall go
    from the wide-wayed
earth back on their way to Olympos,
    forsaking the whole race
200 of mortal men, and all that will be left by them
    to mankind

such force as rapacious hawks,
like our own barons, practice

unashamed

They may live on force, Perses,

not you

you are not strong enough

will be wretched pain. And there shall be no defense
against evil.

Now I will tell you a fable for the barons;
  they understand it.
This is what the hawk said when he had caught
  a nightingale
with spangled neck in his claws and carried her
  high among the clouds.
205 She, spitted on the clawhooks, was wailing pitifully,
  but the hawk, in his masterful manner,
    gave her an answer:
"What is the matter with you? Why scream?
  Your master has you.
You shall go wherever I take you,
  for all your singing.
If I like, I can let you go. If I like,
  I can eat you for dinner.
210 He is a fool who tries to match his strength
  with the stronger.
He will lose his battle, and with the shame
  will be hurt also."
So spoke the hawk, the bird who flies so fast
  on his long wings.

But as for you, Perses, listen to justice;
  do not try to practice
violence; violence is bad for a weak man; even a noble
215 cannot lightly carry the burden of her,
  but she weighs him down
when he loses his way in delusions; that other road
  is the better

(I wonder whether the nobles
really are)

for Justice though often outraged
is stronger in the end

Compare the just community

where people live in what is something
like the Golden Age

which leads toward just dealings. For Justice
  wins over violence
as they come out in the end. The fool knows
  after he's suffered.
The spirit of Oath is one who runs
  beside crooked judgments.

220   There is an outcry when Justice is dragged perforce,
  when bribe-eating
men pull her about, and judge their cases
  with crooked decisions.
She follows perforce, weeping, to the city
  and gatherings of people.
She puts a dark mist upon her and brings a curse
  upon all those
who drive her out, who deal in her
  and twist her in dealing.

225   But when men issue straight decisions
  to their own people
and to strangers, and do not step at all
  off the road of rightness,
their city flourishes, and the people
  blossom inside it.
Peace, who brings boys to manhood, is in their land,
  nor does Zeus
of the wide brows ever ordain that hard war
  shall be with them.

230 Neither famine nor inward disaster comes the way
  of those people
who are straight and just; they do their work
  as if work were a holiday;
the earth gives them great livelihood,
  on their mountains the oaks

with the lawless community

which is like one under a curse

You strong barons, can even you
not understand this?

bear acorns for them in their crowns,
  and bees in their middles.
Their wool-bearing sheep are weighted down
  with fleecy burdens.
235 Their women bear them children 〕 NOT NOW
  who resemble their parents. 〕
They prosper in good things throughout.
  They need have no traffic
with ships, for their own grain-giving land
  yields them its harvest.
    But when men like harsh violence
  and cruel acts, Zeus
of the wide brows, the son of Kronos,
  ordains their punishment.
240 Often a whole city is paid punishment
  for one bad man
who commits crimes and plans reckless action.
  On this man's people
the son of Kronos out of the sky
  inflicts great suffering,
famine and plague together, and the people die
  and diminish.
The women bear children no longer, the houses dwindle
245 by design of Olympian Zeus; or again at other times,
he destroys the wide camped army of a people,
  or wrecks
their city with its walls, or their ships
  on the open water.

You barons also, cannot even you
  understand for yourselves
how justice works? For the immortals
  are close to us, they mingle

The spies of Zeus are everywhere,
though none can see them

and Justice herself informs against
the crooked judges and the takers of
bribes

.

Evil recoils on the evil-doer

250 with men, and are aware of those who
   by crooked decisions
break other men, and care nothing
   for what the gods think of it.
Upon the prospering earth there are
   thirty thousand immortal
spirits, who keep watch for Zeus and all that men do.
They have an eye on decrees given
   and on harsh dealings,
255 and invisible in their dark mist they hover
   on the whole earth.
Justice herself is a young maiden.
   She is Zeus's daughter,
and seemly, and respected by all the gods of Olympos.
When any man uses force on her by false impeachment
she goes and sits at the feet of Zeus Kronion,
   her father,
260 and cries out on the wicked purpose of men,
   so that their people
must pay for the profligacy of their rulers,
   who for their own greedy purposes
twist the courses of justice aslant
   by false proclamations.
Beware, you barons, of such spirits.
   Straighten your decisions
you eaters of bribes. Banish from your minds
   the twisting of justice.

265 The man who does evil to another does evil
   to himself,
and the evil counsel is most evil
   for him who counsels it.

Zeus can see right now what this
very community is doing

Why should I be good if the bad
man will be better off than I?

But I have faith that he will not

Perses, attend

Zeus made brute beasts prey on
each other

But to men alone he gave Justice
and favors the race of those who
prize his gifts

The eye of Zeus sees everything. His mind
　understands all.
He is watching us right now, if he wishes to,
　nor does he fail
to see what kind of justice this community keeps
　inside it.
270　Now, otherwise I would not myself
　be righteous among men
nor have my son be so; for it is a hard thing
　for a man
to be righteous, if the unrighteous man
　is to have the greater right.
But I believe that Zeus of the counsels
　will not let it end thus.

You, Perses, should store away in your mind all
　that I tell you,
275　and listen to justice, and put away
　all notions of violence.
Here is the law, as Zeus established it
　for human beings;
as for fish, and wild animals, and the flying birds,
they feed on each other, since there is no idea
　of justice among them;
but to men he gave justice, and she in the end
　is proved the best thing
280　they have. If a man sees what is right
　and is willing to argue it,
Zeus of the wide brows grants him prosperity.
But when one, knowingly, tells lies and swears
　an oath on it,
when he is so wild as to do incurable damage
　against justice,

There are two roads before us

One is the primrose path to in-
significance
very easy to find and follow

the other is the steep and thorny way
to success

very hard going, up a mountain, but
becomes easy at the summit

The best man is the one who can work
this out for himself
the next best can understand it when
somebody else tells him
You can be the next best man, Perses

Listen to me

this man is left a diminished generation hereafter,
285 but the generation of the true-sworn man
    grows stronger.

I mean you well, Perses, you great idiot,
    and I will tell you.
Look, badness is easy to have, you can take it
    by handfuls
without effort. The road that way is smooth
    and starts here beside you.
But between us and virtue the immortals have put
    what will make us
290 sweat. The road to virtue is long
    and goes steep up hill,
hard climbing at first, but the last of it,
    when you get to the summit
(if you get there) is easy going after the hard part.

That man is all-best who himself works out
    every problem
and solves it, seeing what will be best late
    and in the end.
295 That man, too, is admirable who follows one
    who speaks well.
He who cannot see the truth for himself, nor,
    hearing it from others,
store it away in his mind, that man
    is utterly useless.
As for you, remember what I keep telling you
    over and over:
work, O Perses, illustrious-born, work on,
    so that Famine
300 will avoid you, and august and garlanded Demeter

Gods and men hate the lazy drone
who lives off others so

Work

Idleness is disgrace

so work at what you do best

Poverty brings shame

(the wrong kind, for shame that
means modesty is good)

will be your friend, and fill your barn
  with substance of living;
Famine is the unworking man's most constant
  companion.
Gods and men alike resent that man who, without work
himself, lives the life of the stingless drones,
305 who without working eat away the substance
    of the honeybees'
hard work; your desire, then, should be
  to put your works in order
so that your barns may be stocked with all
  livelihood in its season.
It is from work that men grow rich and own flocks
  and herds;
by work, too, they become much better friends
  of the immortals.
310 [and to men too, for they hate the people
    who do not labor].
Work is no disgrace; the disgrace is in not working;
and if you do work, the lazy man will soon begin
  to be envious
as you grow rich, for with riches go nobility
  and honor.
315 It is best to work, at whatever you have a talent
    for doing,
without turning your greedy thought toward what
  some other man
possesses, but take care of your own livelihood,
  as I advise you.
Shame, the wrong kind of shame, has the needy man
  in convoy,
shame, who does much damage to men,
  but prospers them also,

But you must not escape poverty
by seizing what belongs to others

for that is impiety, like mistreating
your friends and family and the
helpless

and it draws the anger of Zeus

Be pious

shame goes with poverty, but confidence
  goes with prosperity.

320 Goods are not to be grabbed; much better if God
    lets you have them.
  If any man by force of hands wins him
    a great fortune,
  or steals it by the cleverness of his tongue,
    as so often
  happens among people when the intelligence
    is blinded
  by greed, a man's shameless spirit tramples
    his sense of honor;
325 lightly the gods wipe out that man, and diminish
    the household
  of such a one, and his wealth stays with him
    for only a short time.
  It is the same when one does evil to guest
    or suppliant,
  or goes up into the bed of his brother, to lie
    in secret
  love with his brother's wife, doing acts
    that are against nature;
330 or who unfeelingly abuses fatherless children,
  or speaks roughly with intemperate words
    to his failing
  father who stands upon the hateful doorstep
    of old age;
  with all these Zeus in person is angry,
    and in the end
  he makes them pay a bitter price
    for their unrighteous dealings.
335 Keep your frivolous spirit clear of all such actions.

and be religious

day by day

make friends with your neighbors
as well as those to whom you are
bound

As far as you have the power, do sacrifice
   to the immortals,
innocently and cleanly; burn them the shining
   thighbones;
at other times, propitiate them with libations
   and burnings,
when you go to bed, and when the holy light
   goes up the sky;
340 so They may have a complacent feeling and thought
   about you;
so you may buy someone else's land, not have someone
   buy yours.

Invite your friend to dinner; have nothing to do
   with your enemy.
Invite that man particularly who lives close to you.
If anything, which ought not to happen, happens
   in your neighborhood,
345 neighbors come as they are to help; relatives
   dress first.
A bad neighbor's as great a pain as a good one's
   a blessing.
One lucky enough to draw a good neighbor
   draws a great prize.
Not even an ox would be lost, if it were not
   for the bad neighbor.
Take good measure from your neighbor,
   then pay him back fairly
350 with the same measure, or better yet,
   if you can manage it;
so, when you need him some other time,
   you will find him steadfast.

Love those who give

and give, yourself

do not grab

but save, and add to what you have

the habit grows

little by little

but intelligently

No greedy profits; greedy profit is a kind
  of madness.
Be a friend to your friend, and come to him
  who comes to you.
Give to him who gives; do not give to him
  who does not give.
355 We give to the generous man; none gives to him
  who is stingy.
Give is a good girl, but Grab is a bad one;
  what she gives is death.
For when a man gives willingly, though he gives
  a great thing,
yet he has joy of his gift and satisfaction
  in his heart,
while he who gives way to shameless greed and takes
  from another,
360 even though the thing he takes is small,
  yet it stiffens his heart.
For even if you add only a little to a little, yet if
you do it often enough, this little may yet
  become big.
When one adds to what he has,
  he fends off staring hunger.
What is stored away in a man's house
  brings him no trouble.
365 Better for it to be at home, since what is abroad
  does damage.
It is fine to draw on what is on hand, and painful
  to have need
and not have anything there; I warn you
  to be careful in this.
When the bottle has just been opened, and when
  it's giving out, drink deep;

Don't trust anyone, not even your own
brother

and not any woman

Have one son to help the household
If you have more better not die young
(they'll quarrel over the estate)
(or there will not be enough)
but with good seasons there will be
plenty for all
and the more hands the more work done
and work done is the way to prosperity
but the tasks should be done in order
thus:

Begin with the rising of the Pleiades

be sparing when it's half-full; but it's useless
  to spare the fag end.

370   Let the hire that has been promised to a friend
  be made good.
When you deal with your brother, be pleasant,
  but get a witness; for too much
trustfulness, and too much suspicion,
  have proved men's undoing.
    Do not let any sweet-talking woman beguile
  your good sense
with the fascinations of her shape. It's your barn
  she's after.

don't trust women

375 Anyone who will trust a woman is trusting flatterers. *y*
    One single-born son would be right to support

gullible

  his father's
house, for that is the way substance piles up
  in the household;
if you have more than one, you had better live
  to an old age;
yet Zeus can easily provide abundance
  for a greater number,
380 and the more there are, the more work is done,
  and increase increases.
    If the desire within your heart is for greater
  abundance,
do as I tell you: keep on working with work
  and more work.

At the time when the Pleiades, the daughters
  of Atlas, are rising,
begin your harvest, and plow again when they
  are setting.

Work hard and constantly, lose no season

else you may have to go begging
from others
(as you have from me, but I will
give you no more)

and they may not heed you

385   The Pleiades are hidden for forty nights and forty
     days, and then, as the turn of the year reaches
      that point
     they show again, at the time you first sharpen
      your iron.
     This is the usage, whether you live in the plains,
      or whether
     close by the sea, or again in the corners
      of the mountains

390   far away from the sea and its tossing water,
      you have your rich land;
     wherever you live: strip down to sow, and strip
      for plowing,
     and strip for reaping, if you wish to bring in
      the yields of Demeter
     all in their season, and so that each crop
      in its time will increase
     for you; so that in aftertime you may not be in need

395   and go begging to other people's houses,
      and get nothing;
     as you have come now to me; but I will give to you
      no longer;
     no further measure: Perses, you fool, work for it,
     with those works which the gods have arranged
      men shall do,
     lest some day you, with your wife and children,
      in anguish of spirit,

400   have to look to your neighbors for substance,
      and they not heed you.
     Twice you may get help, and three times even,
      but if you plague them
     further, you will get nothing more,
      and your pleading will fall flat.

Make all ready and plan in advance

when the autumn rains come

Your style with words will do you no good; rather,
  I urge you
to work out some way to pay your debts, and escape
  from hunger.

405   First of all, get yourself an ox for plowing,
    and a woman—
for work, not to marry—one who can plow
  with the oxen,
and get all necessary gear in your house
  in good order,
lest you have to ask someone else, and he deny you,
  and you go
short, and the season pass you by, and your work
  be undone.
410   Do not put off until tomorrow and the day after.
A man does not fill his barn by shirking his labors
or putting them off; it is keeping at it that gets
  the work done.
The putter-off of work is the man who wrestles
  with disaster.
    At the time when the force of the cruel sun
  diminishes,
415   and the sultriness and the heat, when powerful Zeus
    brings on
the rains of autumn, and the feel of a man's body
  changes
and he goes much lighter, for at this time
  the star Seirios
goes only a little over the heads
  of hard-fated mankind
in the daytime, and takes a greater part
  of the evening;

choose and cut your wood

.

for wagon and plows

420 at this season, timber that you cut with your ax
    is less open
   to worms, now when it sheds its leaves to the ground,
    and stops sprouting.
   Now, remembering your tasks in their season,
    is your time to cut wood.
   Cut a three-foot length for a mortar and a pestle
    of three cubits,
   and a seven-foot length for an axle; that would be
    quite enough for you,
425 except if you made it eight feet you could cut a maul
    from the end.
   For a wagon of ten palms cut a quarter-felly
    of three spans.
   Cut many curved pieces; and look on the mountain
    and in the meadows,
   for a good piece of holm oak to make your plow-beam,
    and bring it
   home when you find it; this is the strongest
    for plowing oxen,
430 once you have taken it to the carpenter,
    Athene's apprentice,
   and he fixes it in the share and bolts it to the pole
    with dowels.
   You can work the plows in your house,
    and you should have a pair of them,
   one in a single piece, one composite;
    this is the better way,
   for if you break one of them, you can put the oxen
    to the other.
435 Poles of laurel or elm are least likely
    to be worm-eaten.
   The share should be oak, the beam holm oak.

get a pair of seasoned oxen

and a mature, staid hired man

when the cranes go over, plow

(in winter you must feed your oxen,
take care of your gear)

Get yourself two oxen,
  males, nine years old, for their strength
    will be undiminished
and they in full maturity, at their best to work with,
for such a pair will not fight as they drive
    the furrow, and shatter
440 the plow, thus leaving all the work done
    gone for nothing.
And have a forty-year-old man, still young enough,
    to follow
the plow (give him a full four-piece loaf to eat,
    eight ounces);
such a man will keep his mind on his work,
    and drive a straight
furrow, not always looking about for company,
    but keep
445 his thoughts on business. A younger man
    will be no improvement
for scattering the seeds and not piling them
    on top of each other.
A younger man keeps looking for excitement
    with other young people.

At the time when you hear the cry of the crane
    going over, that annual
voice from high in the clouds, you should take notice
    and make plans.
450 She brings the signal for the beginning of planting,
    the winter
season of rains, but she bites the heart
    of the man without oxen.
At this time, keep your horn-curved oxen indoors,
    and feed them.

Plow in the spring too: do not miss
the season: plow your fallow land

Pray

It is easy to make a speech: "Please give me two oxen
and a wagon."
But it's also easy to answer: "I have plenty of work
for my oxen."
455 And a man, rich in his dreams, sees his wagon
as built already,
the idiot, forgetting that the wagon has
a hundred timbers,
and it takes some work to have these laid up at home,
beforehand.
At the first moment when the plowing season
appears for mankind,
set hard to work, your servants, yourself,
everybody together
460 plowing through wet weather and dry
in the plowing season;
rise early and drive the work along, so your fields
will be full.
Plow fallow in spring. Fallow land turned in summer
will not disappoint you.
Fallow land should be sown while the soil
is still light and dry.
Fallow land is kind to children, and keeps off
the hexes.
465 Make your prayers to Zeus of the ground
and holy Demeter
that the sacred yield of Demeter may grow complete,
and be heavy.
Do this when you begin your first planting, when,
gripping the handle
in one hand, you come down hard with the goad
on the backs of your oxen

and sow carefully

and you will be tided over from
season to season

If you wait too long, you will have
a poor harvest

unless the whim of Zeus favors you

as they lean into the pin of the straps.
　　Have a small boy helping you
470　by following and making hard work for the birds
　　with a mattock
covering the seed over. It is best to do things
　　systematically,
since we are only human, and disorder
　　· is our worst enemy.
Do as I tell you, and the ears will
　　sweep the ground in their ripeness,
if the Olympian himself grants that all
　　shall end well;
475　and you can knock the spider-webs from your bins,
　　and, as I hope,
be happy as you draw on all that substance
　　that's stored up.
You will have plenty to make it till the next
　　gray spring; you need not
gaze longingly at others. It's the other man
　　who will need you.
　　　But if you have waited for the winter solstice
　　to plow the divine earth,
480　you will have to squat down to reap, gathering it
　　in thin handfuls,
down in the dust, cross-binding for the looks of it,
　　not very happy;
you will bring it home in a basket,
　　and there will be few to admire you.
Yet still, the mind of Zeus of the aegis changes
　　with changing
occasions, and it is a hard thing for mortal men
　　to figure.

Do not drop in at the smith's fire
to keep warm and gossip in winter

but work

485 Even if you plant late, here is one thing
    that might save you:
at that time when the cuckoo first makes his song
    in the oak leaves,
and across immeasurable earth makes glad
    the hearts of mortals,
if at that time Zeus should rain three days
    without stopping,
and it neither falls short of, nor goes over,
    the height of an ox hoof;
490 then the late planter might come out even
    with the early planter.
Be careful and watch everything well. Let not
    the gray spring
go by unnoticed in her time, nor the rain
    in its season.
    Walk right on past the blacksmith's shop
    with its crowds and its gossip
for warmth, in the winter season, when the cold
    keeps a man from working.
495 A lively man can do much about the house
    in this season.
Winter can be a harsh time of helplessness;
    let it not catch you
in need, as you try to warm a thick foot
    with a thin hand.
The unworking man, who stays on empty anticipation,
needing substance, arranges in his mind
    many bad thoughts,
500 and that is not a good kind of hopefulness
    which is company
for a man who sits, and gossips, and has not enough
    to live on.

(Build barns in summer)

The end of winter is a cold, hard
time

While it is still midsummer, give your people
  their orders.
It will not always be summer. The barns
  had better be building.

Beware of the month Lenaion, bad days,
  that would take the skin off
505 an ox; beware of it, and the frosts, which,
    as Boreas,
the north wind, blows over the land, cruelly develop;
he gets his breath and rises on the open water
  by horse-breeding
Thrace, and blows, and the earth
  and the forest groan, as many
oaks with sweeping foliage, many solid fir trees
510 along the slopes of the mountains his force bends
    against the prospering
earth, and all the innumerable forest
  is loud with him.
The beasts shiver and put their tails
  between their legs, even
those with thick furry coats to cover their hides,
  the cold winds
blow through the furs of even these, for all
  their thickness.
515 The wind goes through the hide of an ox,
  it will not stop him;
it goes through a goatskin, that is fine-haired;
  but not even Boreas'
force can blow through a sheepskin to any degree,
  for the thick fleece
holds him out. It does bend the old man
  like a wheel's timber.

and beasts of the field suffer

Even the deep sea is colder and the
octopus huddles on himself for
warmth

when the sun is gone south from us

and all huddle over like people
bent with age

It does not blow through the soft skin
  of a young maiden
520 who keeps her place inside the house
    by her loving mother
and is not yet initiated in the mysteries of Aphrodite
the golden, who, washing her smooth skin carefully,
  and anointing it
with oil, then goes to bed, closeted
  in an inside chamber
on a winter's day
              that time when old No-Bones the polyp
525 gnaws his own foot in his fireless house,
    that gloomy habitat,
for the sun does not now point him out any range
  to make for
but is making his turns in the countryside
  and population of dusky
men, and is dull to shed his light
  upon Hellenic peoples.
Then all the sleepers in the forest,
  whether horned or hornless,
530 teeth miserably chattering, flee away
    through the mountainous
woods, and in the minds of all
  there is one wish only,
the thought of finding shelter, getting behind
  dense coverts
and the hollow of the rock; then like
  the three-footed individual
with the broken back, and head over, and eyes
  on the ground beneath
535 so doubled, trying to escape the white snow,
    all go wandering.

Dress warm to work

Then you had better cover your skin well,
  as I instruct you.
Put on both a soft outer cloak, and a fringed tunic,
and have an abundant woof woven across a light **warp**;
put this on you, so that your hairs will stay quiet
  in their places
540 and not bristle and stand up shivering
  all over your body.
Upon your feet tie shoes made of the hide
  of a slaughtered
ox; have them fit well, and line them with felt
  on the inside.
Take skins of firstling kids, when the cold season
  is upon you,
and stitch them together with the sinew of an ox,
  for a cape to put over
545 your back, and keep the rain off,
  and on your head you should wear
a hat made out of felt, to keep your ears free
  of the water.
Daybreaks are cold at the time when Boreas
  comes down upon you,
and at dawn there comes down from the starry sky,
  and spreads all over
the land, a mist, helping growth
  for fortunate men's cultivations.
550 This, drawn up from rivers that flow forever,
  and mounting
to a high level over earth on the turn
  of the windstorm,
comes down in the form of rain toward evening
  sometimes, but sometimes

and beat the north wind home

Before spring comes

blows as wind, when Thracian Boreas is chasing
  the thick clouds.
Beat this weather. Finish your work
  and get on homeward
555 before the darkening cloud from the sky
  can gather about you,
and soak your clothing through to the skin,
  leaving you wet through.
Better keep out of its way; of all months
  this is the hardest,
full of stormy weather, hard on flocks,
  hard on people.
At that time the oxen should have half rations,
  but a man
560 more than usual, for the nights add up and are longer.
Keep all these warnings I give you, as the year
  is completed
and the days become equal with the nights again,
  when once more
the earth, mother of us all, bears yield
  in all variety.
    Now, when Zeus has brought to completion
  sixty more winter
565 days, after the sun has turned in his course,
  the star
Arcturus, leaving behind the sacred stream
  of the ocean,
first begins to rise and shine at the edges
  of evening.
After him, the treble-crying swallow,
  Pandion's daughter,
comes into the sight of men when spring's just
  at the beginning.

prune your vines

In late spring the vineyards should
be dug

In harvest time

Wake early, work long

In midsummer when men are burned
out and weakened you can relax
somewhat

570   Be there before her. Prune your vines.
      That way it is better.
       But when House-on-Back, the snail,
     crawls from the ground up
   the plants, escaping the Pleiades, it's no longer
     time for vine-digging;
   time rather to put an edge to your sickles,
     and rout out your helpers.
   Keep away from sitting in the shade or lying in bed
     till the sun's up
575   in the time of the harvest, when the sunshine
     scorches your skin dry.
   This is the season to push your work and bring home
     your harvest;
   get up with the first light so you'll have enough
     to live on.
   Dawn takes away from work a third part
     of the work's measure.
   Dawn sets a man well along on his journey,
     in his work also,
580   dawn, who when she shows, has numerous people going
   their ways; dawn who puts the yoke upon many oxen.
     But when the artichoke is in flower,
    and the clamorous cricket
   sitting in his tree lets go his vociferous singing,
    that issues
   from the beating of his wings, in the exhausting
    season of summer;
585   then is when goats are at their fattest,
     when the wine tastes best,
   women are most lascivious, but the men's strength
    fails them

In the next season, winnow

store your grain

get a new maid

most, for the star Seirios shrivels them, knees
  and heads alike,
and the skin is all dried out in the heat; then,
  at that season,
one might have the shadow under the rock,
  and the wine of Biblis,
590 a curd cake, and all the milk that the goats
  can give you,
the meat of a heifer, bred in the woods,
  who has never borne a calf,
and of baby kids also. Then, too, one can sit
  in the shadow
and drink the bright-shining wine, his heart
  satiated with eating
and face turned in the direction where Zephyros
  blows briskly,
595 make three libations of water from a spring
  that keeps running forever
and has no mud in it; and pour wine
  for the fourth libation.
    Rouse up your slaves to winnow the sacred yield
  of Demeter
at the time when powerful Orion first shows himself;
  do it
in a place where there is a good strong wind,
  on a floor that's rounded.
600 Measure it by storing it neatly away in the bins.
  Then after
you have laid away a good store of livelihood
  in your house,
put your hired man out of doors, and look
  for a serving-maid

look after your beasts and
people

Then in the next season bring in
the grapes

plow again

and your year's back to its
beginning

So much for the landsman's year

with no children, as one with young
  to look after's a nuisance;
and look after your dog with the sharp teeth,
  do not spare feeding him,
605 so the Man Who Sleeps in the Daytime won't be
  getting at your goods.
Bring in hay and fodder so that your mules
  and your oxen
will have enough to eat and go on with. Then,
  when that is done,
let your helpers refresh their knees,
  and unyoke your oxen.
Then, when Orion and Seirios are come to the middle
610 of the sky, and the rosy-fingered Dawn
  confronts Arcturus,
then, Perses, cut off all your grapes, and bring
  them home with you.
Show your grapes to the sun for ten days
  and for ten nights,
cover them with shade for five, and on the sixth day
  press out
the gifts of bountiful Dionysos into jars.
  Then after
615 the Pleiades and the Hyades and the strength of Orion
have set, then remember again to begin
  your seasonal plowing,
and the full year will go underground,
  completing the cycle.

But if the desire for stormy seagoing
  seizes upon you:
why, when the Pleiades, running to escape
  from Orion's

But if, Perses, you must go to sea

(for profit, like our father

who sailed

but finally settled us in this
awful place)

620 grim bulk, duck themselves under the misty face
    of the water,
  at that time the blasts of the winds are blowing
    from every direction,
  then is no time to keep your ships
    on the wine-blue water.
  Think of working your land instead,
    as I keep telling you.
  Haul your ship up on the dry land, and make
    an enclosure
625 of stones about it, to keep out the force of winds
    that blow wet,
  and pull the plug, so the rains of Zeus will not rot
    the timbers.
  Take all the tackle that's rigged to the ship,
    and lay it up indoors,
  neatly stowing the wings of the ship that goes
    over the water;
  hang the well-wrought steering-oar over the smoke
    of the fireplace,
630 and yourself wait for the time to come when a voyage
    is in season.
  Then drag your swift ship down to the sea,
    and put in a cargo
  that will be suitable for it, so you can bring home
    a profit,
  as did my father, and yours too, O Perses,
    you great fool,
  who used to sail in ships, for he wanted to live
    like a noble,
635 and once on a time, leaving Kyme of Aiolis,
    he came here

(the worst place in fact
at the worst time)

though you had better not sail
in the first place

if you must

I will advise you, though I am
no sailor

in his black ship, having crossed over
  a vast amount of water;
and it was not comfort he was fleeing, nor wealth,
  nor prosperity,
but that evil poverty that Zeus gives men
  for a present;
and settled here near Helikon in a hole of a village,
640 Askra, bad in winter, tiresome in summer,
    and good at no season.
    As for you, Perses, remember the timely seasons
  for all work
done, but remember it particularly about seafaring.
Admire a little ship, but put your cargo in a big one.
The bigger the cargo, the bigger will be
  the profit added
645 to profit—if only the winds hold off
    their harsh gales from it.
    But for when, turning your easily blown thoughts
  toward a merchant's
life, you wish to escape your debts,
    and unhappy hunger,
I will show you the measures
  of the much-thundering sea, I
who am not one who has much knowledge of ships
  and sea voyages;
650 for I never did sail in a ship across the wide water
except across to Euboia from Aulis, where once
  the Achaians
stayed out the storm and gathered together
  a great many people
from sacred Hellas to go to Troy,
    the land of fair women.

from inspiration, not experience

The fifty days after the summer
solstice are the best time

There I crossed over to Chalkis
  for the games held in honor
655 of gallant Amphidamas, for the sons
  of this great-hearted
man had set out many chosen prizes. There,
  I can claim,
I won the contest with a song
  and took off an eared tripod;
and this I set up as an offering
  to the Muses of Helikon,
where they first had made me a master
  of melodious singing.
660 This is all my experience with intricately bolted
ships, but still I can tell you the thought,
  which is of aegis-bearing
Zeus, for the Muses have taught me to sing
  immortal poetry.
  For fifty days, after the turn
  of the summer solstice,
when the wearisome season of the hot weather
  goes to its conclusion
665 then is the timely season for men to voyage.
  You will not
break up your ship, nor will the sea drown
  its people, unless
Poseidon, the shaker of the earth,
  of his own volition,
or Zeus, the king of the immortals, wishes
  to destroy it,
for with these rests authority for all outcomes,
  good or evil.
670 At that time the breezes can be judged,
  and the sea is untroubled.

Early spring is dangerous

and death at sea is terrible

At that time, trusting your swift ship to the winds,
  you can draw her
down to the sea at will, and load all your cargo
  inside her;
but make haste still, for the sake of
  an earlier homecoming,
and do not wait for the season of new wine,
  and the autumn
675 rain, and the winter coming on,
  and the hard-blowing southwind
who comes up behind the heavy rains that Zeus sends
  in autumn
and upheaves the sea and makes the open water
  difficult.
   There is one other sailing season for men,
  in spring time.
At that point, when you first make out
  on the topmost branches
680 of the fig tree, a leaf as big as the print
  that a crow makes
when he walks; at that time also the sea is navigable
and this is called the spring sailing season.
  I for my part
do not like it. There is nothing about it
  that I find pleasant.
It's snatched. You will find it hard
  to escape coming to grief. Yet still
685 and even so, men in their short-sightedness
  do undertake it;
for acquisition means life to miserable mortals;
but it is an awful thing to die among the waves.
  No, rather

Only profit can justify the risk

Watch your times

Now, as to your home life

Marry at about thirty, and let her
be about eighteen

and don't be fooled

I tell you to follow with all your attention,
    as I instruct you.
Do not adventure your entire livelihood
    in hollow ships.
690 Leave the greater part ashore and make
    the lesser part cargo.
For it is awful to run on disaster in the waves
    of the open
water, and awful to put an overwhelming load
    on your wagon
and break the axle, and have all the freight
    go to nothing.
Observe measures. Timeliness is best in all matters.

695 You are of age to marry a wife and bring her
    home with you
when you are about thirty, not being many years
    short of
that mark, nor going much over. That age
    is ripe for your marriage.
Let your wife be full grown four years,
    and marry in the fifth.
Better marry a maiden, so you can teach her
    good manners,
700 and in particular marry one who lives close by you.
Look her well over first. Don't marry what will
    make your neighbors
laugh at you, for while there's nothing better
    a man can win him
than a good wife, there's nothing more dismal
    than a bad one.
She eats him out. And even though her husband
    be a strong man,

Be pious

toward gods, family, and friends

Do not make too many friends

Watch your tongue

705   she burns him dry without fire, and gives him
        to a green old age.

Always observe a due regard for the blessed
    immortals.
Do not put some friend on equal terms
    with your brother;
but if you do, never be the first to do him an injury.
Do not tell lies for the sake of talking.
    If your friend begins it
710   by speaking some disagreeable word,
        or doing some injury,
remember, and pay him back twice over. Then,
    if he would bring you
back into his friendship, and propose
    to give reparation,
take him back. A mean man's one
    who is constantly changing
friend for friend. Do not let appearance
    confound perception.
715   Do not be called every man's friend.
      Do not be called friendless,
nor companion of bad people, nor one who quarrels
    with good ones.
     Never be so hard as to mock a man for hateful,
    heart-eating
poverty. That's a gift given
    by the blessed immortals.
The best reserve of resource that men can have
    is a sparing
720   tongue, and they are best liked when that
    goes moderately;

and manners

Be respectful to all gods, including
the powers of nature

Avoid unlucky acts

[if you say a bad thing, you may soon hear a worse] *karma*
  thing said about you.

 Never be disagreeable at a feast
 where many guests
come together; there good feeling's greatest,
 expense is slightest.
 Never, from dawn forward, pour a shining libation
725 of wine to Zeus or the other immortals,
 without washing your hands first.
When you do, they do not hear your prayers;
 they spit them back at you.
 Never stand upright and make water
 facing the sun,
but only, remember, when he has set,
 or before his rising.
Nor do it when you are on the road,
 nor yet turning out from
730 the road, nor showing yourself. For nights
 belong to the Blessed Ones.
A devout man, one who has learned the right way
 to do things,
will huddle down, or go to the wall
 of a courtyard enclosure.
 Do not, when in your house, ever show yourself
 near the hearthside
when you are physically unclean,
 but keep away from it.
735 Do not, when you have come back
 from an ill-omened burial,
beget children, but when you come from a feast
 of the immortals.
 Never wade through the pretty ripples
 of perpetually flowing

such as, for instance, cutting your
nails at a divine service

etc.

rivers, until you have looked at their lovely waters,
  and prayed to them,
and washed your hands in the pale enchanting water.
  For if one
740 wades a river unwashed of hands
    and unwashed of wickedness
the gods are outraged at him, and give him pains
  for the future.

    Never, at a happy festival of the gods, cut off
the dry from the green on the five-branch plant
  with shining iron.

    Never put the wine-ladle on top
  of the mixing bowl
745 when people are drinking. This brings
    accursed bad luck with it.

    Never, when you are building a house,
  leave rough edges on it,
for fear a raucous crow may perch there,
  and croak at you.
Never take up, without an offering, a piece of pottery
and eat or wash from it. There is a forfeit
  on these also.

750   Never let a twelve-year-old boy sit on anything
not to be moved; better not; it makes a man
  lose his virility;
nor a twelve-month-boy either, for this will work
  in the same way.

    A man should never wash his body in water a woman
has used, for there is a dismal forfeit
  that comes in time also
755 for this act.
            Nor, if you chance on sacred offerings
  burning,

Do not gossip

You're starting something you can
not control

Watch what days are lucky or unlucky
for doing what things

and here they are

must you make fun of the rites. The god, naturally,
  resents this.
    Never make water into the outlets
  of rivers meeting
the sea, nor in their springs, but altogether
  avoid this;
nor plunge in them to cool off; it means no good
  if you do this.
760   Do as I tell you. And keep away from
  the gossip of people.
For gossip is an evil thing by nature,
  she's a light weight to lift up,
oh very easy, but heavy to carry, and hard
  to put down again.
Gossip never disappears entirely once many people
have talked her big. In fact, she really is
  some sort of goddess.

765 [Observe the Days that come from Zeus, all]
    in their right order.
Explain them to your workers; that the thirtieth
  of the month
is best for supervising works,
  and for doling provisions.
    And here follow the days that come to us
  from the counselor
Zeus, when men who judge their true nature
  can observe them.
770   First of all, the first, fourth, and seventh
  of the month are holy;
it was on this last that Leto gave birth to Apollo
of the golden sword. Then the eighth and ninth,
  two days in each month

(according to the waxing month, the
midmonth, and the waning month)

(or to the two halves of the month)

(or according to the whole month)

as it waxes, are excellent for mortal labors.
The eleventh day, and the twelfth too,
    are both very good days
775 either for shearing sheep or for reaping
    the good harvest;
but of these the twelfth day is far better
    than the eleventh,
for it is on the twelfth that the air-flying
    spider weaves
her web in the full of the day, and Know-All, the ant,
    piles her dirt-hill.
On this day a wife could set up her loom
    and get her work going.
780   In the waxing month, the thirteenth day
    is to be avoided
for planting seed, but it is the best
    for transplanting seedlings.
    The sixth of midmonth is very unfavorable
    for plants,
but good for the birth of males; not favorable
    for girl-children,
either to be born in the first place or to go
    to their marriage.
785 Nor is the early sixth either suitable
    for a girl-child
to be born, but for gelding kids, and lambs,
    and for putting
an enclosure around the sheeppen
    it is a day kind and propitious.
Fine, too, for a boy born; but he'll be one
    who is fond of teasing,
and telling lies, and flattering speeches,
    and beguiling sweet talk.

790 On the eighth of the month, it is time
  to geld the boar and the bellowing
 bull; but the hard-working mules should be done
  on the twelfth day.
  On the great twentieth, in full day,
  a man who will be learned
 should be born, for one of that day
  is well armed with brains.
 The tenth is fine for a boy-child to be born;
  for a girl-child
795 the fourth of midmonth, on which day
  you should gentle your sheep, your
 horn-curved shambling cattle, sharp-toothed dog,
  and hard-working
 mules, by stroking them with the hand,
  but be very careful
 on the fourth of the waxing, the fourth
  of the waning month, to avoid
 troubles that eat out the heart. For this day
  has great authority.
800 On the fourth day of the month
  bring your wife home, only
 first watch out the bird signs most favorable
  to this business.
  Beware of all fifth days; they are harsh
  and angry; it was on
 the fifth, they say, that the Erinyes
  assisted at the bearing
 of Oath, whom Strife bore, to be a plague
  on those who take false oath.
805 On the seventh of midmonth, after looking
  carefully all about you,

Observe these properties of days
It is the final observance
necessary to make your life of
work a happy one

throw down the holy grain of Demeter
on a well-rounded
floor; and it's time for the carpenter
to cut the house beams
and all the many timbers that are required
for ship building.
On the fourth, one can begin putting
the narrow ships together.

810   The ninth of midmonth grows better toward evening.
The first ninth is altogether free of harm for men,
for it is a very good day for either a man or a woman
either to beget or be born. It is never
a truly bad day.
   Few know that the twenty-seventh of the month
is the best day

815 for starting on a wine jar or for putting the yoke
on the necks
of oxen, or of mules, or swift-footed horses, also
for hauling a fast ship with many locks
down to the wine-blue
waters. For there are few who call true things
by their right names.
   On the fourth open a wine jar; the fourth
is surpassingly sacred

820 in midmonth. Few, again, know that any day
after the twentieth
is best in the dawning, but in the late day
it grows less good.

   These are the days which greatly advantage
earthly people.
The others are full of vain noise, ineffective,
and produce nothing.

Every man will have his favorite day, but few
  know about them.
825 A certain day is sometimes a stepmother,
  sometimes a mother.
But that man is fortunate and blessed who,
  knowing all these
matters, goes on with his work,
  innocent toward the immortals,
watching all the bird signs, and keeping clear
  of transgression.

Theogony

Let us begin our singing
  from the Helikonian Muses
who possess the great and holy mountain
  of Helikon
and dance there on soft feet
  by the dark blue water
of the spring, and by the altar
  of the powerful son of Kronos;
5 who wash their tender bodies in the waters
  of Permessos
or Hippokrene, spring of the Horse,
  or holy Olmeios,
and on the high places of Helikon
  have ordered their dances
which are handsome and beguiling,
  and light are the feet they move on.
From there they rise, and put a veiling
  of deep mist upon them,
10 and walk in the night, singing
  in sweet voices, and celebrating
Zeus, the holder of the aegis, and Hera,
  his lady
of Argos, who treads on golden sandals,
  and singing also
Athene the gray-eyed, daughter of Zeus
  of the aegis,
Phoibos Apollo, and Artemis
  of the showering arrows,
15 Poseidon who encircles the earth in his arms
  and shakes it,
stately Themis, and Aphrodite
  of the fluttering eyelids,
Hebe of the golden wreath, beautiful Dione,

Leto and Iapetos and devious-devising Kronos,
Eos, the dawn, great Helios,
  and shining Selene,

20 Gaia, the earth, and great Okeanos,
  and dark Night,
and all the holy rest of the everlasting
  immortals.
And it was they who once taught Hesiod
  his splendid singing
as he was shepherding his lambs
  on holy Helikon,
and these were the first words of all
  the goddesses spoke to me,

25 the Muses of Olympia, daughters of Zeus
  of the aegis:
"You shepherds of the wilderness, poor fools,
  nothing but bellies,
we know how to say many false things
  that seem like true sayings,
but we know also how to speak the truth
  when we wish to."
  So they spoke, these mistresses of words,
  daughters of great Zeus,

30 and they broke off and handed me a staff
  of strong-growing
olive shoot, a wonderful thing;
  they breathed a voice into me,
and power to sing the story of things
  of the future, and things past.
They told me to sing the race
  of the blessed gods everlasting,
but always to put themselves
  at the beginning and end of my singing.

35   But what is all this to me, the story
        of the oak or the boulder?

      Come you then, let us begin from the Muses,
        who by their singing
      delight the great mind of Zeus, their father,
        who lives on Olympos,
      as they tell of what is, and what is to be,
        and what was before now
      with harmonious voices, and the sound
        that comes sweet from their mouths
40   never falters, and all the mansion of Zeus
        the father
      of the deep thunder is joyful
          in the light voice of the goddesses
      that scatters through it, and the peaks
        of snowy Olympos re-echo
      and the homes of the immortals, and they
        in divine utterance
      sing first the glory of the majestic race
        of immortals
45   from its beginning, those born
        to wide Ouranos and Gaia,
      and the gods who were born to these in turn,
        the givers of blessings.
      Then next they sing of Zeus, the father
        of gods and of mortals,
      and they begin this strain and end
        this strain singing of him,
      how greatly he surpasses all gods,
        and in might is the strongest.
50   And then again the Olympian Muses,
        daughters of aegis-

wearing Zeus, delight his mind that dwells
  on Olympos
by singing the race of human kind,
  and the powerful Giants.
    Mnemosyne, queen of the Eleutherian hills,
  bore them
in Pieria, when she had lain
  with the Kronian Father;
55   they bring forgetfulness of sorrows,
  and rest from anxieties.
For nine nights Zeus of the counsels
  lay with her, going
up into her sacred bed, far away
  from the other immortals.
But when it was a year,
  after the seasons' turning
and the months had waned away, and many days
  were accomplished,
60   she bore her nine daughters, concordant
  of heart, and singing
is all the thought that is in them,
  and no care troubles their spirits.
She bore them a little way off
  from the highest snowy summit
of Olympos; there are their shining
  dancing places, their handsome
houses, and the Graces and Desire live there
  beside them
65   in festivity; lovely is the voice
  that issues from their lips
as they sing of all the laws and all
  the gracious customs

of the immortals, and glorify them
  with their sweet voices.
At that time, glorying in their power
  of song, they went to Olympos
in immortal music, and all the black earth
  re-echoed to them
70 as they sang, and the lovely beat
  of their footsteps sprang beneath them
as they hastened to their father, to him
  who is King in the heaven,
who holds in his own hands the thunder
  and the flamy lightning,
who overpowered and put down
  his father Kronos, and ordained
to the immortals all rights that are theirs,
  and defined their stations.
75   All these things the Muses who have
  their homes on Olympos
sang then, and they are nine daughters
  whose father is great Zeus:
Kleio and Euterpe, Thaleia and Melpomene,
Terpsichore and Erato, Polymnia and Ourania,
with Kalliope, who of all holds
  the highest position.
80 For it is she who attends
  on the respected barons.
And when on one of these kingly nobles,
  at the time of his birth,
the daughters of great Zeus cast their eyes
  and bestow their favors,
upon his speech they make a distillation
  of sweetness,

and from his mouth the words run blandishing,
  and his people
85 all look in his direction as he judges
    their cases
with straight decisions, and,
    by an unfaltering declaration
can put a quick and expert end even
    to a great quarrel:
and that is why there are temperate barons,
    because for their people
who have gone astray in assembly these
    lightly turn back their actions
90 to the right direction, talking them over
    with gentle arguments.
As such a one walks through an assembly,
    the people adore him
like a god, with gentle respect;
    he stands out among all assembled.
Such is the holy gift the Muses
    give to humanity.
So it is from the Muses, and from Apollo
    of the far cast,
95 that there are men on earth who are poets,
    and players on the lyre.
The lords are from Zeus; but blessed
    is that one whom the Muses
love, for the voice of his mouth runs
    and is sweet, and even
when a man has sorrow fresh
    in the troublement of his spirit
and is struck to wonder over the grief
    in his heart, the singer,

100 the servant of the Muses singing
    the glories of ancient
men, and the blessed gods
    who have their homes on Olympos,
makes him presently forget his cares,
    he no longer remembers
sorrow, for the gifts of the goddesses
    soon turn his thoughts elsewhere.

Hail, then, children of Zeus:
    grant me lovely singing.

105 Now sound out the holy stock
    of the everlasting immortals
who came into being out of Gaia
    and starry Ouranos
and gloomy Night, whom Pontos, the salt sea,
    brought to maturity;
and tell, how at the first the gods
    and the earth were begotten
and rivers, and the boundless sea,
    raging in its swell,
110 the blazing stars, and the wide sky above all,
    tell of
the gods, bestowers of blessings,
    who were begotten of all these,
and how they divided their riches
    and distributed their privileges,
and how they first took possession
    of many-folded Olympos,
tell me all this, you Muses
    who have your homes on Olympos,

115 from the beginning, and tell who was first
    to come forth among them.
     First of all there came Chaos,
    and after him came
Gaia of the broad breast,
    to be the unshakable foundation
of all the immortals who keep the crests
    of snowy Olympos,
and Tartaros the foggy in the pit
    of the wide-wayed earth,
120 and Eros, who is love, handsomest among all
    the immortals,
who breaks the limbs' strength,
    who in all gods, in all human beings
overpowers the intelligence in the breast,
    and all their shrewd planning.
From Chaos was born Erebos, the dark,
    and black Night,
and from Night again Aither and Hemera,
    the day, were begotten,
125 for she lay in love with Erebos
    and conceived and bore these two.
But Gaia's first born was one
    who matched her every dimension,
Ouranos, the starry sky,
    to cover her all over,
to be an unshakable standing-place
    for the blessed immortals.
Then she brought forth the tall Hills,
    those wild haunts that are beloved
130 by the goddess Nymphs who live on the hills
    and in their forests.

Without any sweet act of love
  she produced the barren
sea, Pontos, seething in his fury of waves,
  and after this
she lay with Ouranos, and bore him
  deep-swirling Okeanos
the ocean-stream; and Koios, Krios,
  Hyperion, Iapetos,
135 and Theia too and Rheia, and Themis,
  and Mnemosyne,
Phoibe of the wreath of gold,
  and Tethys the lovely.
After these her youngest-born
  was devious-devising Kronos,
most terrible of her children;
  and he hated his strong father.
    She brought forth also the Kyklopes,
  whose hearts are proud and powerful,
140 Brontes and Steropes, and Arges
  of the violent spirit,
who made the thunder and gave it to Zeus,
  and fashioned the lightning.
These in all the rest of their shape
  were made like gods,
but they had only one eye set in the middle
  of their foreheads.
Kyklopes, wheel-eyed, was the name given them,
  by reason
145 of the single wheel-shaped eye
  that was set in their foreheads.
Strength and force, and contriving skills,
  were in all their labors.

And still other children were born
  to Gaia and Ouranos,
three sons, big and powerful, so great
  they could never be told of,
Kottos, Briareos, and Gyes,
  overmastering children.

150 Each had a hundred intolerably strong arms
    bursting
out of his shoulders,
  and on the shoulders of each grew fifty
heads, above their massive bodies;
  irresistible
and staunch strength matched the appearance
  of their big bodies,
and of all children ever born
  to Gaia and Ouranos

155 these were the most terrible,
  and they hated their father
from the beginning, and every time each one
  was beginning
to come out, he would push them back again,
  deep inside Gaia,
and would not let them into the light,
  and Ouranos exulted
in his wicked work; but great Gaia
  groaned within for pressure

160 of pain; and then she thought of an evil,
  treacherous attack.
Presently creating the element of gray flint
she made of it a great sickle,
  and explained it to her own children,
and spoke, in the disturbance of her heart,
  to encourage them:

"My sons, born to me of a criminal father,
  if you are willing
165 to obey me, we can punish your father
    for the brutal treatment
he put upon you, for he was first to think
  of shameful dealing."
    So she spoke, but fear took hold of all,
  nor did one of them
speak, but then great devious-devising Kronos
  took courage
and spoke in return,
  and gave his gracious mother an answer:
170 "My mother, I will promise to undertake
    to accomplish
this act, and for our father,
  him of the evil name, I care
nothing, for he was the first
  to think of shameful dealing."
    So he spoke, and giant Gaia
  rejoiced greatly in her heart
and took and hid him in a secret ambush,
  and put into his hands
175 the sickle, edged like teeth, and told him
    all her treachery.
And huge Ouranos came on
  bringing night with him, and desiring
love he embraced Gaia and lay over her
  stretched out
complete, and from his hiding place his son
  reached with his left hand
and seized him, and holding in his right
  the enormous sickle

180 with its long blade edged like teeth,
 he swung it sharply,
and lopped the members of his own father,
 and threw them behind him
to fall where they would,
 but they were not lost away when they were flung
from his hand, but all the bloody drops
 that went splashing from them
were taken in by Gaia, the earth,
 and with the turning of the seasons
185 she brought forth the powerful Furies
 and the tall Giants
shining in their armor
 and holding long spears in their hands;
and the nymphs they call, on boundless earth,
 the Nymphs of the Ash Trees.
But the members themselves, when Kronos
 had lopped them with the flint,
he threw from the mainland
 into the great wash of the sea water
190 and they drifted a great while
 on the open sea, and there spread
a circle of white foam
 from the immortal flesh, and in it
grew a girl, whose course first took her
 to holy Kythera,
and from there she afterward made her way
 to sea-washed Cyprus
and stepped ashore, a modest lovely Goddess,
 and about her
195 light and slender feet the grass grew,
 and the gods call her

Aphrodite, and men do too,
  and the aphro-foam-born
goddess, and garlanded Kythereia,
  because from the seafoam
she grew, and Kythereia because she had gone
  to Kythera,
and Kyprogeneia, because she came forth
  from wave-washed Cyprus,
200 and Philommedea, because she appeared
  from *medea*, members.
And Eros went with her, and handsome Himeros
  attended her
when first she was born, and when she joined
  the immortal community,
and here is the privilege she was given
  and holds from the beginning,
and which is the part she plays among men
  and the gods immortal:
205 the whispering together of girls,
  the smiles and deceptions,
the delight, and the sweetnesses of love,
  and the flattery.
    But their great father Ouranos,
  who himself begot them,
bitterly gave to those others, his sons,
  the name of Titans,
the Stretchers, for they stretched
  their power outrageously and accomplished
210 a monstrous thing, and they would some day
  be punished for it.

But Night bore horrible Moros, and black Ker,
  End and Fate,

and Death, and Sleep, and she bore also
  the brood of Dreams,
she, dark Night, by herself,
  and had not been loved by any god,
and then again she bore mocking Momos
  and painful Oizys,
215 and the Hesperides, who across
    the fabulous stream of the Ocean
keep the golden apples
  and the fruit-bearing orchards,
and she bore the destinies, the Moirai,
  and the cruelly never-forgetful
Fates, Klotho, Lachesis, and Atropos,
  who at their birth
bestow upon mortals their portion
  of good and evil,
220 and these control the transgressions
    of both men and divinities,
and these goddesses never remit
  their dreaded anger
until whoever has done wrong
  gives them satisfaction.
And she, destructive Night, bore Nemesis,
  who gives much pain
to mortals; and afterward cheating Deception
  and loving Affection
225 and then malignant Old Age
    and overbearing Discord.
    Hateful Discord in turn
    bore painful Hardship,
and Forgetfulness, and Starvation,
  and the Pains, full of weeping,

the Battles and the Quarrels, the Murders
  and the Manslaughters,
the Grievances, the lying Stories,
  the Disputations,
230 and Lawlessness and Ruin, who share
  one another's nature,
and Oath, who does more damage than any other
  to earthly
men, when anyone, of his knowledge,
  swears to a false oath.
  But Pontos, the great Sea, was father
  of truthful Nereus
who tells no lies, eldest of his sons.
  They call him the Old Gentleman
235 because he is trustworthy, and gentle,
  and never forgetful
of what is right, but the thoughts
  of his mind are mild and righteous.
And Pontos again fathered great Thaumas,
  and haughty Phorkys
when he lay with Gaia, and he fathered Keto
  of the fair face,
and Eurybia, who has a heart of stone
  inside her.
240 To Nereus and to Doris of the lovely hair,
  daughter
of Okeanos the completely encircling river,
  there were born
in the barren sea daughters
  greatly beautiful even among goddesses:
Ploto and Eukrante and Amphitrite and Saö,
Eudora and Thetis, and Galene and Glauke,
245 Kymothoë and Speio, and Thoë and lovely Halia,

Pasithea and Erato, Eunike of the rose arms,
and graceful Melite and Eulimene and Agauë,
Doto and Proto, Dynamene and Pherousa,
Nesaië and Aktaië and Protomedeia,
250   Doris and Panopeia, and Galateia
    the beautiful,
Hippothoë the lovely
    and Hipponoë of the rose arms,
Kymodoke who, with Kymatolege and Amphitrite,
light of foot, on the misty face
    of the open water
easily stills the waves and hushes the winds
    in their blowing,
255   Kymo and Eïone, Halimede
    of the bright garland,
Glaukonome, the lover of laughter,
    and Pontoporeia,
Leagore and Euagore and Laomedeia,
Poulynoë and Autonoë and Lysianassa,
Euarne of the lovely figure
    and face of perfection,
260   Psamathe of the graceful form
    and shining Menippe,
Neso and Eupompe, and Themisto and Pronoë,
and Nemertes, whose mind is like that
    of her immortal father.
These were the daughters born
    to irreproachable Nereus,
fifty in all, and the actions they know
    are beyond reproach, also.
265   Now Thaumas married a daughter
    of deep-running Okeanos,

Elektra, and she bore him swift-footed Iris,
  the rainbow,
and the Harpies of the lovely hair,
  Okypete and Aëllo,
and these two in the speed of their wings
  keep pace with the blowing
winds, or birds in flight, as they soar
  and swoop, high aloft.
270   And to Phorkys Keto bore the Graiai,
  with fair faces
and gray from birth, and these the gods
  who are immortal
and men who walk on the earth call Graiai,
  the gray sisters,
Pemphredo robed in beauty and Enyo
  robed in saffron,
and the Gorgons who, beyond the famous stream
  of the Ocean,
275 live in the utmost place toward night,
  by the singing Hesperides:
they are Sthenno, Euryale, and Medusa,
  whose fate was a sad one,
for she was mortal, but the other two
  immortal and ageless
both alike. Poseidon, he of the dark hair,
  lay with
one of these, in a soft meadow
  and among spring flowers.
280 But when Perseus had cut off
  the head of Medusa
there sprang from her blood great Chrysaör
  and the horse Pegasos

so named from the *pegai*, the springs
  of the Ocean, where she was born,
while Chrysaör is named from the golden *aör*,
  the sword he handles.
Pegasos, soaring, left the earth,
  the mother of sheepflocks,
285 and came to the immortals, and there he lives
  in the household
of Zeus, and carries the thunder
  and lightning for Zeus of the counsels.
Chrysaör, married to Kallirhoë,
  daughter of glorious
Okeanos, was father
  to the triple-headed Geryon,
but Geryon was killed by the great strength
  of Herakles
290 at sea-circled Erytheia
  beside his own shambling cattle
on that day when Herakles drove
  those broad-faced cattle
toward holy Tiryns, when he crossed
  the stream of the Ocean
and had killed Orthos and the oxherd Eurytion
out in that gloomy meadow
  beyond the fabulous Ocean.
295   But she, Kallirhoë, bore another
  unmanageable monster
like nothing human
  nor like the immortal gods either,
in a hollow cave. This was the divine
  and haughty Echidna,
and half of her is a nymph
  with a fair face and eyes glancing,

but the other half is a monstrous snake,
  terrible, enormous
300 and squirming and voracious,
  there in earth's secret places.
For there she has her cave
  on the underside of a hollow
rock, far from the immortal gods,
  and far from all mortals.
There the gods ordained her a fabulous home
  to live in
which she keeps underground among the Arimoi,
  grisly Echidna,
305 a nymph who never dies, and all her days
  she is ageless.
    They say that Typhaön, the terrible,
  violent and lawless,
was joined in love with this girl
  of the glancing eyes, and she
conceiving bore children to him,
  with hard tempers.
First she bore him Orthos,
  who was Geryones' herding dog,
310 and next again she bore the unspeakable,
  unmanageable
Kerberos, the savage,
  the bronze-barking dog of Hades,
fifty-headed, and powerful,
  and without pity.
And third again she bore
  the grisly-minded Hydra
of Lerna, whom the goddess
  white-armed Hera nourished

315 because of her quenchless grudge
    against the strong Herakles.
Yet he, Herakles, son of Zeus,
    of the line of Amphitryon,
by design of Athene the spoiler,
    and with help from warlike
Iolaos, killed this beast
    with the pitiless bronze sword.
Hydra bore the Chimaira, who snorted
    raging fire,
320 a beast great and terrible,
    and strong and swift-footed.
Her heads were three: one was that
    of a glare-eyed lion,
one of a goat, and the third of a snake,
    a powerful dragon.
325 But Chimaira was killed by Pegasos
    and gallant Bellerophon.
But Echidna also, in love with Orthos,
    mothered the deadly
Sphinx, the bane of the Kadmeians,
    and the Nemeian Lion
whom Hera, the queenly wife of Zeus,
    trained up and settled
among the hills of Nemeia,
    to be a plague to mankind.
330 There he preyed upon the tribes
    of the indwelling people,
and was as a King over Tretos
    and Apesas and Nemeia.
Nevertheless, the force of strong Herakles
    subdued him.

Keto, joined in love with Phorkys,
mothered the youngest
of the deadly snakes, that one who
at the gloomy great hidden
335 limits of the Earth guards
the all-golden apples.
This snake is of the generation
of Keto and Phorkys.
   Tethys bore to Okeanos the swirling Rivers,
Neilos the Nile, Alpheios,
and deep-eddying Eridanos,
Strymon and Maiandros, Istros
of the beautiful waters,
340 Phasis and Rhesos
and silver-swirling Acheloios,
Nessos and Rhodios, Heptaporos
and Haliakmon,
Grenikos and Aisepos, and Simoeis,
who is godlike,
Hermos and Peneios,
and Kaïkos strongly flowing,
and great Sangarios, and Ladon,
and Parthenios,
345 Euenos and Ardeskos, and Skamandros,
who is holy.
   She brought forth also a race apart
of daughters, who with
Lord Apollo and the Rivers have the young
in their keeping
all over the earth, since this right
from Zeus is given them.
They are Peitho, Admete, Ianthe and Elektra,
350 Doris and Prymno and Ourania like a goddess,

Hippo and Klymene, Rhodeia and Kallirhoë,
Zeuxo and Klytia, and Idyia and Pasithoë,
Plexaura and Galaxaura and lovely Dione,
Melobosis and Thoë, and Polydora the shapely,
355   Kerkeïs of the lovely stature,
    and ox-eyed Plouto,
Xanthe and Akaste, Perseïs and Ianeira,
Petraïë the lovely, and Menestho, and Europa,
Metis and Eurynome, Telesto robed in saffron,
Chryseïs, and Asia, and alluring Kalypso,
360   Eudora and Tyche, and Amphiro and Okyroë,
  and Styx, who among them all
    has the greatest eminence.
Now these are the eldest of the daughters
  who were born to Tethys
and Okeanos, but there are many others
  beside these,
for there are three thousand
  light-stepping daughters of the Ocean
365   scattered far and wide, bright children
  among the goddesses, and all
alike look after the earth
  and the depths of the standing water;
and as many again are the rest of the Rivers,
  murmurously running,
sons of Okeanos and the lady Tethys
  was their mother,
and it would be hard for a mortal man
  to tell the names
370   of all of them; but each is known
  by those who live by him.
    Theia brought forth great Helios
  and shining Selene

the Sun and Moon, and Eos the Dawn,
  who lights all earthly
creatures, and the immortal gods
  who hold the wide heaven.
These she brought forth, being subdued
  in love to Hyperion.
375   Eurybia, shining among the goddesses,
  was joined in love
with Krios, and brought forth
  the great Astraios and Pallas
and Perses, who shines among all
  for his intelligence.
    Eos, a goddess couched in love with a god,
  brought forth
to Astraios the strong-spirited winds,
  Zephyros
380 the brightener, Boreas of the headlong track,
  and Notos.
After these she, Erigeneia,
  bore Eosphoros, the dawnstar,
and all those other shining stars
  that are wreathed in the heaven.
    And Styx, daughter of Okeanos,
  lying in love with Pallas,
bore in their halls Rivalry
  and sweet-stepping Victory,
385 and also Power and Force,
  who are her conspicuous children,
and these have no home that is not the home
  of Zeus, no resting
place nor road, except where that god
  has guided them,

but always they are housed by Zeus
  of the heavy thunder.
For this was the will of Styx,
  that Okeanid never-perishing,
390 on the day when the Olympian flinger
    of the lightning
summoned all the immortal gods
  to tall Olympos
and said that any god who fought on his side
  with the Titans
should never be beaten out of his privilege,
  but each should maintain
the position he had had before
  among the immortals; he said, too,
395 that the god who under Kronos
    had gone without position or privilege
should under him be raised to these,
  according to justice.
And Styx the imperishable was first
  to come to Olympos
bringing her children, as her own father
  had advised her.
Zeus gave her position,
  and gave her great gifts further,
400 for he established her to be the oath
    of the immortals,
and that her children all their days
  should live in his household.
And so, as he had promised, in every way
  he fulfilled it
throughout. But he himself keeps
  the great power, and is master.

Now, Phoibe in turn went into the bed
of love with Koios,
405 a goddess with a god, and there
through his love she conceived
and bore Leto of the dark robe,
a sweet goddess always,
kind to mortal men
and to the immortal divinities,
sweet from the beginning,
the gentlest of all who are on Olympos.
She bore also renowned Asteria, whom on a day
410 Perses led home to his great house,
to be called his true wife,
and she conceiving bore Hekate, whom Zeus,
son of Kronos,
honored above all others,
for he gave her gifts that were glorious,
to have a part of the earth as hers,
and a part of the barren
sea, and she, with a place also
in the starry heaven,
415 is thus exalted exceedingly
even among the immortals.
For even now, whenever any one
of mortal men makes
a handsome sacrifice in propitiation,
according to usage,
he invokes Hekate, and recompense abundant
and lightly granted
befalls that man whose prayers
the goddess receives with favor,
420 and she grants him good success,
for hers is the power to do this.

For among the children who were born
  to Ouranos and Gaia
and had station allotted,
  among all these she has a certain office.
Nor did the son of Kronos use violence
  toward her nor deprive her
of the rights she had among Titan gods
  of the older generation

425 but she holds her apportioned share
  as formerly from the beginning,

427 nor, because she is an only child,
  does the goddess have the less honor,

426 and a privileged place in the earth,
  and in the sky, and the sea also;
but as much as others and far more,
  seeing that Zeus honors her.
She greatly assists and advantages any man,
  as she pleases, and in

430 the assembly of the people a man shines
  when she wishes it,
and when men put on their armor
  to go to battle, where men
are wasted, the goddess
  is present there also, to give out
the victory and the glory
  to whichever side she wishes.
And she sits beside solemn kings when they give
  their judgment.

435 She is great, too,
  where men contend in athletics,
and there the goddess stands by those
  whom she will, and assists them,

and one who, by his force and strength,
  has won a fine prize,
lightly and gladly carries it home,
  and brings glory to his parents.
She is great also in standing by the riders
  as she wishes,
440 and those who on the gray-green,
    the hard-wracking sea, make a living,
and they pray to Hekate
  and to the deep-thunderous Earthshaker,
and lightly the high goddess
  grants a great haul of fish, and lightly
too she takes it away when it has shown,
  if such is her pleasure.
She is great in the farms also
  to help Hermes swell the produce,
445 and the driven herds of cattle
    and the wide-ranging goat flocks
and the flocks of deep-fleeced sheep,
  all these also at her own pleasure
she weightens to many out of few,
  or makes few out of many.
Thus, though she is only the single child
  of her mother
she is honored with high offices
  among all the immortals.
450 Zeus son of Kronos made her, too,
    protector of those children
who after her laid eyes on the Dawn,
  the many-light-beaming;
so she, from the beginning,
  has protected children, and these are her offices.

Rheia, submissive in love to Kronos,
  bore glorious children,
Histia and Demeter,
  Hera of the golden sandals,
455 and strong Hades, who under the ground
  lives in his palace
and has a heart without pity;
  the deep-thunderous Earthshaker,
and Zeus of the counsels,
  who is the father of gods and of mortals,
and underneath whose thunder
  the whole wide earth shudders;
but, as each of these children
  came from the womb of its mother
460 to her knees, great Kronos swallowed it down,
  with the intention
that no other of the proud children
  of the line of Ouranos
should ever hold the king's position
  among the immortals.
For he had heard, from Gaia
  and from starry Ouranos,
that it had been ordained for him,
  for all his great strength,
465 to be beaten by his son,
  and through the designs of great Zeus.
Therefore he kept watch, and did not sleep,
  but waited
for his children, and swallowed them,
  and Rheia's sorrow was beyond forgetting.
But when she was about to bear Zeus,
  the father of mortals

and gods, then Rheia went
  and entreated her own dear parents,
470 and these were Gaia and starry Ouranos,
    to think of some plan
  by which, when she gave birth to her dear son,
    the thing might not
  be known, and the fury of revenge
    be on devious-devising Kronos
  the great, for his father,
    and his own children whom he had swallowed.
  They listened gladly
    to their beloved daughter, and consented,
475 and explained to her
    all that had been appointed to happen
  concerning Kronos, who was King, and his son,
    of the powerful
  spirit, and sent her to Lyktos,
    in the fertile countryside of Crete
  at that time when she was to bring forth
    the youngest of her children,
  great Zeus; and the Earth, gigantic Gaia,
    took him inside her
480 in wide Crete, there to keep him alive
    and raise him.
  There Earth arrived
    through the running black night, carrying
  him, and came first to Lyktos,
    and holding him in her arms, hid him
  in a cave in a cliff, deep in
    under the secret places
  of earth, in Mount Aigaion
    which is covered with forest.

485 She wrapped a great stone in baby-clothes,
     and this she presented
   to the high lord, son of Ouranos,
     who once ruled the immortals,
   and he took it then in his hands
     and crammed it down in his belly,
   hard wretch, nor saw in his own mind
     how there had been left him
   instead of the stone a son,
     invincible and unshakable
490 for the days to come, who soon by force
     and his hands defeating him
   must drive him from his title,
     and then be lord over the immortals.
       And presently after this the shining limbs
       and the power
   of the lord, Zeus, grew great,
     and with the years circling on
   great Kronos, the devious-devising,
     fooled by the resourceful
495 promptings of Gaia, once again
     brought up his progeny.
   First he vomited up the stone,
     which last he had swallowed,
   and this Zeus took and planted in place,
     on earth of the wide ways,
   at holy Pytho, in the hollow ravines
     under Parnassos,
500 to be a portent and a wonder
     to mortal men thereafter.
   Then he set free from their dismal bonds
     the brothers of his father,

the sons of Ouranos, whom his father
  in his wild temper had enchained,
and they remembered, and knew gratitude
  for the good he had done them,
and they gave him the thunder,
  and the smoky bolt, and the flash
505 of the lightning, which Gaia the gigantic
  had hidden till then.
With these to support him, he is lord
  over immortals and mortals.

Iapetos took Klymene,
  the light-stepping daughter of Ocean,
to be his wife, and mounted into the same bed
  with her,
510 and she bore him a son, Atlas,
  of the powerful spirit,
and she bore him high-vaunting Menoitios,
  and Prometheus
of the intricate and twisting mind,
  and Epimetheus
the gullible, who from the beginning
  brought bad luck to men
who eat bread, for he first accepted
  from Zeus the girl Zeus fashioned
and married her.
            Menoitios was mutinous,
  and Zeus of the wide brows
515 struck him with the blazing thunderbolt
  and dropped him to Erebos
because of his too-great hardihood
  and outrageous action.

But Atlas, under strong constraint,
  at earth's uttermost
places, near the sweet-singing Hesperides,
  standing upright
props the wide sky upon his head
  and his hands never wearied,
520 for this was the doom
  which Zeus of the counsels dealt out to him.
And in ineluctable, painful bonds
  he fastened Prometheus
of the subtle mind, for he drove a stanchion
  through his middle. Also
he let loose on him the wing-spread eagle,
  and it was feeding
on his imperishable liver, which by night
  would grow back
525 to size from what the spread-winged bird
  had eaten in the daytime.
But Herakles, the powerful son
  of lightfooted Alkmene,
killed the eagle
  and drove that pestilential affliction
from Iapetos' son, and set him free
  from all his unhappiness,
not without the will of high-minded Zeus
  of Olympos
530 in order that the reputation
  of Thebes-born Herakles
might be greater even than it had been
  on the earth that feeds many.
With such thoughts in mind he honored his son
  and made him glorious,

and angry as he had been before,
 he gave up his anger;
for Prometheus once had matched wits
 against the great son of Kronos.
535 It was when gods, and mortal men,
 took their separate positions
at Mekone, and Prometheus,
 eager to try his wits, cut up
a great ox, and set it before Zeus,
 to see if he could outguess him.
He took the meaty parts and the inwards
 thick with fat, and set them
before men, hiding them away
 in an ox's stomach,
540 but the white bones of the ox he arranged,
 with careful deception,
inside a concealing fold of white fat,
 and set it before Zeus.
At last the father of gods
 and men spoke to him, saying:
"Son of Iapetos, conspicuous among all Kings,
old friend, oh how prejudicially
 you divided the portions."
545 So Zeus, who knows imperishable counsels,
 spoke in displeasure,
but Prometheus the devious-deviser,
 lightly smiling,
answered him again, quite well aware
 of his artful deception:
"Zeus most high, most honored
 among the gods everlasting,
choose whichever of these the heart within
 would have you."

550 He spoke, with intent to deceive, and Zeus,
    who knows imperishable
counsels, saw it, the trick
    did not escape him, he imagined
evils for mortal men in his mind,
    and meant to fulfil them.
In both his hands he took up the portion
    of the white fat. Anger
rose up about his heart
    and the spite mounted in his spirit
555 when he saw the white bones of the ox
    in deceptive arrangement.

Ever since that time the races of mortal men
    on earth have burned
the white bones to the immortals
    on the smoky altars.

Then Zeus the cloud-gatherer
    in great vexation said to him:
"Son of Iapetos, versed in planning
    beyond all others,
560 old friend, so after all you did not forget
    your treachery."
    So Zeus, who knows imperishable counsels,
    spoke in his anger,
and ever remembering this deception
    thereafter, he would not
give the force of weariless fire
    to the ash-tree people,
not to people who inhabit the earth
    and are mortal,

565 no, but the strong son of Iapetos
    outwitted him
and stole the far-seen glory
    of weariless fire, hiding it
in the hollow fennel stalk;
    this bit deep into the feeling
of Zeus who thunders on high,
    and it galled the heart inside him
when he saw the far-seen glory of fire
    among mortal people,
570 and next, for the price of the fire,
    he made an evil thing for mankind.
For the renowned smith of the strong arms
    took earth, and molded it,
through Zeus's plans, into the likeness
    of a modest young girl,
and the goddess gray-eyed Athene
    dressed her and decked her
in silverish clothing, and over her head
    she held, with her hands,
575 an intricately wrought veil in place,
    a wonder to look at,
and over this on her head
    she placed a wreath of gold, one
that the very renowned smith
    of the strong arms had fashioned
580 working it out with his hands,
    as a favor to Zeus the father.
On this had been done much intricate work,
    a wonder to look at:
wild animals, such as the mainland
    and the sea also produce

in numbers, and he put many on,
  the imitations of living
things, that have voices, wonderful,
  and it flashed in its beauty.
585   But when, to replace good,
  he had made this beautiful evil
thing, he led her out
  where the rest of the gods and mortals
were, in the pride and glory
  that the gray-eyed daughter of a great
father had given; wonder
  seized both immortals and mortals
as they gazed on this sheer deception,
  more than mortals can deal with.
590 For from her originates the breed
  of female women,
and they live with mortal men,
  and are a great sorrow to them,
and hateful poverty they will not share,
  but only luxury.
As when, inside the overarching hives,
  the honeybees
595 feed their drones (and these are accomplished
  in doing no good,
while the bees, all day long
  until the sun goes down
do their daily hard work
  and set the white combs in order,
and the drones, spending their time
  inside the hollow skeps,
garner the hard work of others
  into their own bellies),

600   so Zeus of the high thunder established women,
      for mortal
    men an evil thing,
      and they are accomplished in bringing
    hard labors.
               And Zeus made, in place
      of the good, yet another evil.
    For whoever, escaping marriage
      and the sorrowful things women do,
    is unwilling to marry, must come then
      to a mournful old age
605   bereft of one to look after it,
      and in need of livelihood
    lives on, and when he dies
      the widow-inheritors divide up
    what he has. While if the way of marriage
      befalls one
    and he gets himself a good wife,
      one with ways suited to him,
    even so through his lifetime the evil remains,
      balancing
610   the good, and he whose luck
      is to have cantankerous children
    lives keeping inside him discomfort
      which will not leave him
    in heart and mind; and for this evil
      there is no healing.
      So it is not possible to hide
      from the mind of Zeus, nor escape it;
    for not even the son of Iapetos,
      the gentle Prometheus,
615   was able to elude that heavy anger,
      but, for all his

numerous shifts, force
  and the mighty chain confine him.
    Now, when Ouranos their father
    was bitter at heart against Obriareos
  and Kottos and Gyes (because he was so struck
    by their towering
  vigor, and their stature and beauty),
    therefore he bound them
620 in strong bonds, and settled them
    under the wide-wayed earth. There
  dwellers under the ground
    and with a life full of agony
  they lived at the uttermost end,
    at the edges of the great earth,
  with a long spell of grieving,
    and at their hearts a great sorrow;
  but Zeus son of Kronos,
    and the other immortal divinities
625 whom Rheia of the fair tresses
    had born in love to Kronos,
  brought them back to the light
    again at the instigation of Gaia.
  For Gaia had told the gods the whole truth,
    from the beginning,
  that with these Three victory would be won,
    and glorious honor.
  For a long time now, the Titan gods
    and those who were descended
630 from Kronos had fought each other,
    with hard heart-hurting struggles,
  ranged in opposition
    all through the hard encounters:

one side, the haughty Titans,
   fought from towering Othrys,
but they of the other side, the gods,
   the givers of good things,
whom Rheia bore in love to Kronos,
   these fought from Olympos.
635   These then, with heart-hurting rancor
     against each other, fought
for ten full years, continually,
   nor was there any
release from the hardship of hostility,
   nor any end to it
for either side, and the balance
   of the fighting was even. But after
Zeus had given the Three Gods all they wished
   and needed,
640   ambrosia and nectar, which the very gods
     themselves feed on,
then the bold spirit rose up again
   in the hearts of all three,
when they had eaten of the nectar
   and delightful ambrosia.
Then to these three spoke the father of gods
   and of mortals:
"Hear me, O shining children
   of Ouranos and Gaia
645   while I speak out what the heart
     in my breast commands me.
All our days, the Titan gods and we,
   who were born
of Kronos, have been fighting
   a long time now, in opposed

battle, for the sake of victory and power.
  Now, therefore,
show yourselves against the Titans
  in the grim encounter,
650 and show the greatness of your strength,
  your hands irresistible;
remember the love we gave you, the kindness,
  how you had been treated
before you came back into the light
  out of cruel bondage,
and out from under the gloom and the mist,
  all through our contriving."
    So he spoke, and in turn unfaulted Kottos
    answered him:
655 "What need to speak, what you say
  is not unknown. We ourselves
know it, your counsels and perception
  are beyond all others,
that you are the immortals' defender
  against stark ruin.
For it is only by your forethought
  we ever came back up
again from the gloom and the mist
  and from that merciless bondage,
660 through you, O lord, son of Kronos,
  when we suffered what we never had looked for.
Therefore now, with stubborn spirit
  and resolute purpose
we shall be defenders of your power
  in the grim encounter
and fight against the Titans
  in the strong shock of battle."

    So he spoke, and the gods,
      the givers of blessings, assented
665 as they heard what he said,
      and the spirit in them was insistent on battle
    more even than it had been,
      and they launched an unwelcome onset
    all, the female and the male gods alike,
      on that day,
    and the Titan gods, and those
      of the generation of Kronos,
    and those whom Zeus had upraised
      from under the earth and Erebos
670 back to the light, fierce gods and mighty,
      with strength overmastering.
    Each and all alike had a hundred strong arms
      bursting
    out of his shoulders, and on the shoulders
      of each grew fifty
    heads above their massive bodies,
      and now at this time
    these stood forth against the Titans
      in bitter combat
675 wielding in their ponderous hands
      steep cliffside boulders,
    while on the opposite side the Titans
      stiffened their battalions
    in eager courage, and the work of force
      and hands was conspicuous
    on either side, and the infinite great sea
      moaned terribly
    and the earth crashed aloud,
      and the wide sky resounded

680 as it was shaken, and tall Olympos rocked
    on its bases
in the fan of the wind of the immortals,
    and a strong shudder drove deep
into gloomy Tartaros under the suddenness
    of the footrush
and the quenchless crashing of their feet
    and their powerful missiles.
So either against either they threw
    their re-echoing weapons
685 and the noise of either side outcrying
    went up to the starry
heaven as with great war crying
    they drove at each other.
    Now Zeus no longer held in his strength,
    but here his heart filled
deep with fury, and now he showed
    his violence entire
and indiscriminately. Out of the sky
    and off Olympos
690 he moved flashing his fires incessantly,
    and the thunderbolts,
the crashing of them and the blaze
    together came flying, one after
another, from his ponderous hand,
    and spinning whirls of inhuman
flame, and with it the earth,
    the giver of life, cried out
aloud as she burned, and the vast forests
    in the fire screamed.
695 All earth was boiling with it,
    and the courses of the Ocean

and the barren sea, and the steam
  and the heat of it was engulfing
the Titans of the earth, while the flames
  went up to the bright sky
unquenchably, and the blaze
  and the glare of thunder and lightning
blinded the eyes of the Titan gods,
  for all they were mighty.
700 The wonderful conflagration crushed Chaos,
  and to the eyes' seeing
and ears' hearing the clamor of it,
  it absolutely
would have seemed as if Earth
  and the wide Heaven above her
had collided, for such would have been
  the crash arising
as Earth wrecked and the sky came piling down
  on top of her,
705 so vast was the crash heard
  as the gods collided in battle.
The winds brought on with their roaring
  a quake of the earth and dust storm,
with thunder and with lightning,
  and the blazing thunderbolt,
the weapons thrown by great Zeus,
  and they carried the clamor
and outcry between the hosts opposed,
  and a horrible tumult
710 of grisly battle uprose,
  and both sides showed power in the fighting.
Then the battle turned; before that,
  both sides attacking

in the fury of their rage fought on
   through the strong encounters.
    But now the Three, Kottos and Briareos
   and Gyes,
insatiate of battle, stirred
   the grim fighting in the foremost,
715 for from their powerful hands they volleyed
   three hundred boulders
one after another, and their missile flights
   overwhelmed the Titans
in darkness, and these they drove
   underneath the wide-wayed
earth, and fastened them there
   in painful bondage, for now they
had beaten the Titan gods with their hands,
   for all their high hearts.
720 They drove them as far underground
   as earth is distant from heaven.
Such is the distance from earth's surface
   to gloomy Tartaros.
For a brazen anvil dropping out of the sky
   would take nine
nights, and nine days, and land on earth
   on the tenth day,
and a brazen anvil dropping off the earth
   would take nine
725 nights, and nine days, and land in Tartaros
   on the tenth day.

A wall of bronze is driven around it,
   and night is drifted
about its throat in a triple circlet,
   while upward from it

there grow and branch the roots of the earth,
  and of the barren sea.
There the Titan gods live buried
  under the darkness
730 and the mists, and this is by the decree
  of Zeus the cloud-gatherer,
in a moldy place, at the uttermost edges
  of monstrous
earth. There is no way out for them;
  Poseidon has fitted
brazen doors, and the walls run around
  enclosing everything.
And there Gyes, Kottos,
  and great-hearted Briareos
735 are settled as faithful sentinels
  for Zeus of the aegis.
    And there, for the gloomy earth,
  and for Tartaros of the mists,
and for the barren great sea
  and the starry heaven,
for all these, the springs
  and the sources stand there, all in order;
an unpleasant, moldy place,
  and even the gods loathe it;
740 it is a great chasm, and once
  one were inside the gates of it
within a whole year's completion
  he would not come to the bottom,
but stormblast on cruel stormblast
  would sweep him one way
and another; this is a monstrous place,
  and even the immortals

fear it. And here stand the terrible houses
  of dark Night,
745 and the buildings are sheathed in the dark
  of the clouds. Before them
Atlas, son of Iapetos, stands
  staunchly upholding
the wide heaven upon his head
  and with arms unwearying
sustains it, there where Night and Day
  come close to each other
and speak a word of greeting
  and cross on the great threshold
750 of bronze, for the one is coming back in
  and the other is going
outdoors, and the house never at once
  contains both of them,
but at every time, while one of them
  is out of the house, faring
over the length of the earth,
  the other remaining indoors
waits for the time of her own journey,
  when the other one comes back;
755 the one carries for people on earth Light
  the far-flashing,
while the other one carries Sleep
  in her arms, and he is Death's brother,
and she is Night, the destructive,
  veiled in a cloud of vapor.
    And there the children of Night
  the gloomy have their houses.
These are Sleep and Death, dread divinities.
  Never upon them

760 does Helios, the shining sun,
    cast the light of his eye-beams,
neither when he goes up the sky
    nor comes down from it.
One of these, across the earth
    and the wide sea-ridges,
goes his way quietly back and forth,
    and is kind to mortals,
but the heart of the other one is iron,
    and brazen feelings
765 without pity are inside his breast.
    When he takes hold of anyone
he keeps him; and even the immortal gods
    hate this one.
    And there, at the front, stand
    the resounding halls of the Earth gods,
of Hades the powerful,
    and of august Persephone,
there they stand, and before them
    a dreaded hound, on watch,
770 who has no pity, but a vile stratagem:
    as people go in
he fawns on all, with actions of his tail
    and both ears,
but he will not let them go back out,
    but lies in wait for them
and eats them up, when he catches any
    going back through the gates.
775   And there is housed a goddess
    loathed even by the immortals:
dreaded Styx, eldest daughter of Ocean,
    who flows back

on himself, and apart from the gods
   she lives in her famous palace
which is overroofed with towering rocks,
   and the whole circuit
is undergirded with silver columns,
   and pushes heaven;
780 and seldom does the daughter of Thaumas,
   fleet-footed Iris,
come her way with a message
   across the sea's wide ridges,
those times when dispute and quarreling
   start among the immortals,
and some one of those who have their homes
   on Olympos is lying,
and Zeus sends Iris
   to carry the many-storied water
785 that the gods swear their great oath on,
   thence, in a golden pitcher,
that cold water that drizzles down
   from a steep sky-climbing
cliffside, and it is one horn
   of the Ocean stream, and travels
off that holy river a great course
   through night's blackness
under the wide-wayed earth,
   and this water is a tenth part
790 of all, for in nine loops
   of silver-swirling waters, around
the earth and the sea's wide ridges
   he tumbles into salt water,
but this stream, greatly vexing the gods,
   runs off the precipice.

And whoever of the gods,
   who keep the summits of snowy
Olympos, pours of this water,
   and swears on it, and is forsworn,
795 is laid flat, and does not breathe,
   until a year is completed;
nor is this god let come near ambrosia
   and nectar
to eat, but with no voice in him,
   and no breath, he is laid out
flat, on a made bed, and the evil coma
   covers him.
But when, in the course of a great year,
   he is over his sickness,
800 there follows on in succession another trial,
   yet harsher:
for nine years he is cut off
   from all part of the everlasting
gods, nor has anything to do
   with their counsels, their festivals
for nine years entire, but in the tenth
   he once more mingles
in the assemblies of the gods
   who have their homes on Olympos.
805 Such an oath did the gods make
   of the imperishable, primeval
water of Styx; and it jets down
   through jagged country.
   And there, for the gloomy earth,
   and for Tartaros of the mists,
and for the barren great sea
   and the starry heaven,

for all these the springs and sources
  stand there, all in order;
810 an unpleasant, moldy place,
  and even the gods loathe it.
And there are the marmoreal gates,
  and the brazen threshold
self-ongrown, unshakable,
  and gripped on to branching
roots, and in front of it,
  and apart from all the immortals,
are settled the Titans, the other side
  of gloomy Chaos;
815 only the glorious helpers of Zeus,
  the loud-crashing,
are settled in houses along the foundations
  of the Ocean:
Kottos and Gyes, that is;
  but of strong-grown Briareos
the deep-stroking shaker of the Earth,
  Poseidon, made
a son-in-law, and married him to Kymopoleia,
  his daughter.

820   Now after Zeus had driven the Titans
  out of heaven,
gigantic Gaia, in love with Tartaros,
  by means of golden
Aphrodite, bore the youngest of her children,
  Typhoeus;
the hands and arms of him are mighty,
  and have work in them,
and the feet of the powerful god
  were tireless, and up from his shoulders

825 there grew a hundred snake heads,
    those of a dreaded dragon,
    and the heads licked with dark tongues,
    and from the eyes on
    the inhuman heads fire glittered
    from under the eyelids:
    from all his heads fire flared
    from his eyes' glancing;
    and inside each one of these horrible heads
    there were voices
830 that threw out every sort of horrible sound,
    for sometimes
    it was speech such as the gods
    could understand, but at other
    times, the sound of a bellowing bull,
    proud-eyed and furious
    beyond holding, or again like a lion
    shameless in cruelty,
    or again it was like the barking of dogs,
    a wonder to listen to,
835 or again he would whistle
    so the tall mountains re-echoed to it.
    And now that day there would have been done
    a thing past mending,
    and he, Typhoeus, would have been master
    of gods and of mortals,
    had not the father of gods and men
    been sharp to perceive it
    and gave a hard, heavy clap of thunder,
    so that the earth
840 gave grisly reverberation,
    and the wide heaven above, and

the sea, and the streams of Ocean,
 and the underground chambers.
And great Olympos was shaken
 under the immortal feet
of the master as he moved,
 and the earth groaned beneath him,
and the heat and blaze from both of them
 was on the dark-faced sea,
845 from the thunder and lightning of Zeus
 and from the flame of the monster,
from his blazing bolts and from the scorch
 and breath of his stormwinds,
and all the ground and the sky
 and the sea boiled, and towering
waves were tossing and beating all up
 and down the promontories
in the wind of these immortals,
 and a great shaking of the earth
850 came on, and Hades, lord over
 the perished dead, trembled,
and the Titans under Tartaros,
 who live beside Kronos,
trembled to the dread encounter
 and the unending clamor.
But now, when Zeus had headed up
 his own strength, seizing
his weapons, thunder, lightning,
 and the glowering thunderbolt,
855 he made a leap from Olympos, and struck,
 setting fire
to all those wonderful heads set about
 on the dreaded monster.

Then, when Zeus had put him down
   with his strokes, Typhoeus
crashed, crippled, and the gigantic earth
   groaned beneath him,
and the flame from the great lord
   so thunder-smitten ran out
860 along the darkening and steep forests
   of the mountains
as he was struck, and a great part
   of the gigantic earth burned
in the wonderful wind of his heat,
   and melted, as tin melts
in the heat of the carefully grooved crucible
   when craftsmen
work it, or as iron, though that is
   the strongest substance,
865 melts under stress of blazing fire
   in the mountain forests
worked by handicraft of Hephaistos
   inside the divine earth.
So earth melted in the flash
   of the blazing fire; but Zeus
in tumult of anger cast Typhoeus
   into broad Tartaros.

   And from Typhoeus comes the force of winds
   blowing wetly:
870 all but Notos, Boreas, and clearing Zephyros,
   for their generation is of the gods,
      they are a great blessing
   to men, but the rest of them blow wildly
      across the water
   and burst upon the misty face
      of the open sea, bringing

heavy distress to mortal men,
   and rage in malignant
875 storm, and blow from veering directions,
   and scatter the shipping
and drown the sailors,
   and there is no remedy against this evil
for men who run into such winds
   as these on the open water.
And then again, across the limitless
   and flowering
earth, they ruin the beloved works
   of ground-dwelling people
880 by overwhelming them with dust
   and hard tornadoes.

Now when the immortal gods had finished
   their work of fighting,
they forced the Titans to share with them
   their titles and privilege.
Then, by the advice of Gaia,
   they promoted Zeus, the Olympian
of the wide brows, to be King
   and to rule over the immortals
885 and he distributed among them their titles
   and privilege.

Zeus, as King of the gods,
   took as his first wife Metis,
and she knew more than all the gods
   or mortal people.
But when she was about to be delivered
   of the goddess, gray-eyed

Athene, then Zeus, deceiving her perception
  by treachery
890 and by slippery speeches,
  put her away inside his own belly.
This was by the advices of Gaia,
  and starry Ouranos,
for so they counseled,
  in order that no other everlasting
god, beside Zeus, should ever be given
  the kingly position.
For it had been arranged that, from her,
  children surpassing in wisdom
895 should be born, first the gray-eyed girl,
  the Tritogeneia
Athene; and she is the equal of her father
  in wise counsel
and strength; but then a son to be King
  over gods and mortals
was to be born of her, and his heart
  would be overmastering:
but before this, Zeus put her away
  inside his own belly
900 so that this goddess should think for him,
  for good and for evil.
    Next Zeus took to himself Themis,
  the shining, who bore him the Seasons,
Lawfulness, and Justice,
  and prospering Peacetime: these
are concerned to oversee the actions
  of mortal people;
and the Fates, to whom Zeus of the counsels
  gave the highest position:

905 they are Klotho, Lachesis, and Atropos:
    they distribute
to mortal people what people have,
    for good and for evil.
    Eurynome, daughter of Okeanos,
    lovely in appearance,
bore to Zeus the three Graces
    with fair cheeks; these are
Aglaia and Euphrosyne and lovely Thalia,
910 and from the glancing of their lidded eyes
    bewildering
love distills; there is beauty
    in their glance, from beneath brows.
    Zeus entered also into the bed
    of fruitful Demeter,
who bore him Persephone of the white arms,
    she that Aïdoneus
ravished away from her mother,
    and Zeus of the counsels granted it.
915   Then again, he loved Mnemosyne,
    of the splendid tresses,
from whom were born to him the Muses
    with veils of gold, the Nine
whose pleasure is all delightfulness,
    and the sweetness of singing.
    Leto, who had lain in the arms of Zeus
    of the aegis,
bore Apollo, and Artemis
    of the showering arrows,
920 children more delightful than all
    the other Ouranians.
    Last of all, Zeus took Hera
    to be his fresh consort,

and she, lying in the arms
  of the father of gods and mortals,
conceived and bore Hebe to him, and Ares,
  and Eileithyia.
  Then from his head, by himself,
  he produced Athene of the gray eyes,
925 great goddess, weariless,
  waker of battle noise, leader of armies,
a goddess queen who delights in war cries,
  onslaughts, and battles,
while Hera, without any act of love,
  brought forth glorious
Hephaistos, for she was angered
  and quarreling with her husband;
and Hephaistos in arts and crafts
  surpasses all the Ouranians.

[Now Hera was angered, and quarreled
  with her husband, and because
of this quarrel she herself brought forth a glorious son
Hephaistos, without any act of love-making
  with Zeus of the aegis;
but he, apart from Hera, had lain in love with a fair-faced
daughter of Okeanos and lovely-haired Tethys,
Metis, whom he deceived,
  for all she was so resourceful,
for he snatched her up in his hands
  and put her inside his belly
for fear that she might bring forth
  a thunderbolt stronger than his own;
therefore the son of Kronos, who dwells high,
  seated in the bright air,

swallowed her down of a sudden,
  but she then conceived Pallas
Athene, but the father of gods
  and men gave birth to her
near the summit of Triton
  beside the banks of the river.
But Metis herself, hidden away
  under the vitals of Zeus,
stayed there; she was Athene's mother;
  worker of right actions,
beyond all the gods
  and beyond all mortal people in knowledge;
and there Athene had given to her hands
  what made her supreme
over all other immortals who have
  their homes on Olympos;
for Metis made the armor of Athene,
  terror of armies,
in which Athene was born
  with her panoply of war upon her.]

930 From Amphitrite and Poseidon,
  loud-thundering earth shaker,
was born great Triton, widely powerful,
  he who, sustaining
the sea's basis, beside his dear mother
  and the lord his father,
dwells in the golden house, a dreaded god.
                                    Now Kythereia
  to Ares, stabber of shields, bore Panic
  and Terror, dreaded
935 gods, who batter the dense battalions
  of men embattled

in horrible war, they with Ares,
  sacker of cities. She also
bore him Harmonia, she whom high-spirited
  Kadmos married.
    Maia, daughter of Atlas,
  mounted the sacred bed
of Zeus, and bore Hermes the good,
  the herald of the immortals.
940   Semele, daughter of Kadmos,
  lay in love with Zeus also
and bore him a glorious son, Dionysos,
  giver of good things,
she mortal, he immortal,
  but now both are gods together.
Alkmene, lying in love with Zeus
  who gathers the clouds,
bore him powerful Herakles.
945   Hephaistos, of the high renown
  and the strong arms, took
Aglaia, youngest of the Graces,
  to be his fresh wife.
    Dionysos, he of the golden hair,
  took blonde Ariadne,
daughter of Minos, to be his blossoming wife,
  and Kronian
Zeus caused her likewise to be immortal
  and ageless.
950   Herakles, the strong and courageous son
  of light-stepping
Alkmene, after he had completed
  his sorrowful labors,
took the daughter of great Zeus
  and Hera of the golden

sandals, Hebe, as his modest wife
on snowy Olympos,
blessed he, who having ended his long work,
lives now
955 among the immortals, without sorrow,
ageless all his days always.
To Helios, the unwearied Sun,
the glorious daughter
of Okeanos, Perseïs, bore Circe
and the King Aietes,
and Aietes, son of Helios
who pours his light on mortals,
married, by the counsels of the gods,
the fair-faced
960 daughter of Okeanos, the terminal river,
Idyia, who, subdued to him in love,
and through golden
Aphrodite, bore him Medeia of the slim ankles.

Farewell now, you who have your homes
on Olympos, farewell
to islands, mainland masses,
and the open sea that is between them.
965 But now, O sweet-spoken Muses of Olympos,
daughters
of Zeus of the aegis,
sing out now the names of those goddesses
who went to bed with mortal men and,
themselves immortal,
bore to these children in the likeness
of the immortals.
Demeter, shining among goddesses,
after the embraces

970 of the hero Iasion in the sweetness of love,
    brought forth Ploutos
in a three-times-plowed field
    there in the fertile countryside
of Crete, a good son, who walks over earth
    and the sea's wide ridges
everywhere, and he who meets him
    with the giving of hands between them
is made a prosperous man,
    to whom great wealth is granted.
975   To Kadmos, Harmonia,
    daughter of Aphrodite the golden,
bore Ino, and Semele, and Agaüe of the fair face,
and Autonoë, who was taken to wife
    by Aristaios
of the deep hair, and Polydoros,
    in high-crowned Thebes.
Kallirhoë, daughter of Okeanos,
    lying in the embraces
980 of powerful-minded Chrysaör,
    through Aphrodite the golden
bore him a son, most powerful
    of all men mortal,
Geryones, whom Herakles
    in his great strength killed
over his dragfoot cattle
    in water-washed Erytheia.
    To Tithonos, Eos the Dawn bore Memnon
    of the brazen
985 helm, king of Ethiopians,
    and the lord Emathion.
Then, embraced by Kephalos,
    she engendered a son, glorious

Phaethon, the strong, a man in the likeness
  of the immortals;
and, while he still had the soft flower
  of the splendor of youth upon him,
still thought the light thoughts of a child,
  Aphrodite, lover of laughter,
990 swooped down and caught him away
  and set him in her holy temple
to be her nocturnal temple-keeper,
  a bright divinity.
    Jason, the son of Aison, by counsel
  of the everlasting
gods, took Medeia, daughter of Aietes
  King under god's hand,
and led her from Aietes' house,
  having completed the many
995 painful trials that the great, proud king,
  Pelias, had imposed
upon him, for he was oppressive,
  hardhearted and heavy-handed,
but Jason did all, and came back to Iolkos,
  after much suffering,
and brought back with him on the fast ship
  the girl of the glancing
eyes, Medeia, and made her
  his blossoming wife, and she
1000 submitting in love to Jason,
  shepherd of the people, bore him
a son, Medeios, and Cheiron
  the son of Philyra fostered him
on the mountains, and so the purpose
  of mighty Zeus was accomplished.

But of the daughters of Nereus,
the old man of the sea, one,
Psamathe, shining among goddesses,
joined to Aiakos
1005   in love through golden Aphrodite,
bore him Phokos,
while Thetis, she of the silver feet,
submitting to Peleus
bore him Achilleus, the lion-hearted,
breaker of warriors.
Kythereia of the garlands joining
in love's delight
with the hero Anchises, bore him Aineias,
among the forests
1010   and many-folded valleys of the peaks of Ida.
Circe, daughter of Helios, who is the son
of Hyperion,
was joined in love
with hardy-minded Odysseus, and bore him
Agrios and Latinos,
a man faultless and powerful,
[and also, through golden Aphrodite,
bore him Telegonos],
1015   and these far, far away in the uttermost,
magical islands
were Kings over the Tyrsenians,
of glorious reputation.
Kalypso, shining among goddesses,
joining in love's
delight with Odysseus, bore him Nausithoös
and Nausinoös.
These went to bed with mortal men and,
themselves immortal,

1020   bore to them children in the likeness
     of the immortals.

But now, O sweet-spoken Muses of Olympos,
  daughters
of Zeus of the aegis,
  sing out the generation of women.

Like her . . . or like her . . . or like her
  who . . .

the Shield of Herakles

Or like her who, leaving her house
  and the land of her fathers,
came to Thebes, in the company
  of warlike Amphitryon;
she, Alkmene, daughter of the leader of men,
  Elektryon;
she who, for stature and beauty,
  surpassed all the generation
5 of female women; and for intellect also
    she had no rival
among any of those who, mortal themselves,
  lay with mortals, and bore them
children; and from her head
  and her dark eyes there was
a blowing grace, as if it were
  from Aphrodite the golden.
But for all this, she in her mind
  was devoted to her own
10 husband, as no other of womankind
    ever was devoted.
Now he, overpowering him, had killed
  her excellent father
in a quarrel over cattle,
  and so leaving his own country
came as suppliant to Thebes
  and to the shield-armored Kadmeians.
And there he had his house, and lived,
  with his modest, wedded
15 wife; but without the sweet delight of love,
    for he was not
allowed to go into the bed
  of Elektryon's light-stepping daughter

until he should avenge the murder
　of his wife's high-hearted
brothers, and with ravening fire
　burn up the villages
of fighting men and heroes,
　Taphians and Teleboans.
20　Such had been his agreement,
　and the gods had been witnesses to it,
and the thought of their anger
　was in his mind, yet he was hastening
to get the great work done
　that Zeus had imposed upon him
as soon as might be, and with him,
　longing for battle and fighting,
went the Boiotians, lashers-on of horses,
　breathing fury under
25　their shields, and the Lokrians
　who fight at close quarters, and the high-hearted
Phokians, and at the head of all
　the big son of Alkaios
glorying in his people. Meanwhile,
　the father of gods and mortals
was weaving another design in his mind,
　how, both for gods
and for men who eat bread,
　he might plant a protector against destruction.
30　He rose up from Olympos, mulling over
　in the mind his deception,
for he wanted the love
　of the well-girt woman. He went
by night. Presently he came to Typhaonion,
　and from

there Zeus of the counsels
  lighted on top of Sphinx Hill,
and there sat down and thought out
  the wonders he would put into action;
35 for that very night
  he lay with Elektryon's daughter, lady
of light walking, in love and in bed,
  and all his desire was accomplished,
and that same night Amphitryon,
  leader of men, a glorious
hero, came back to his own house,
  with his own work accomplished,
and would make no move
  to see his serving men, nor his shepherds
40 of the countryside, until he had gone to bed
  with his wife, for such
was the longing in the heart of Amphitryon,
  the shepherd of the people.
And, as when a man, to his great delight,
  has escaped the hardship
of some hard-wearing sickness,
  or from strong constraint of imprisonment,
so now Amphitryon, having wound up
  his hard assignment, came
45 full of delight and love
  back into his own household,
and there, nightlong, he lay in the arms
  of his modest wife
reveling in the delights given by Aphrodite
  the golden,
and the lady, submitting to the god,
  and to the man far best

of men in Thebes of the seven gates,
  bore twin sons
50   whose hearts and spirits were not alike;
  it is true they were brothers,
but the one was a lesser man,
  and the other a man far greater,
a dread man and strong, Herakles the powerful.
  This one
she conceived under the embraces of Zeus,
  the dark clouded,
but the other one, Iphikles,
  to Amphitryon of the restless
55   spear; seed that was separate;
  one lying with a mortal man
and one with Zeus, son of Kronos,
  marshal of all the immortals.

It was he, Herakles, who killed Kyknos,
  high-hearted son of Ares,
for he came upon him in the precinct
  of Apollo, who strikes from afar,
himself and his father, Ares
  insatiable in battle, blazing
60   both of them like the light of burning fire
  in their armor
and standing in their chariots,
  and their running horses trampled
and dented the ground with their hooves,
  and the dust swirled up around them,
beaten up between the compacted chariot
  and the feet of the horses,
and the well-put-together chariots
  and their rails clattered

65 to the gallop of the straining horses,
  and handsome Kyknos was joyful
in his hope of slaughtering the warlike son
  of Zeus with the bronze
spear, and his driver with him,
  and stripping their glorious armor;
but Phoibos Apollo would not listen
  to his prayers and promises,
since he himself had set powerful Herakles
  against him.
70 And all the grove
  and the altar of Pagasaian Apollo
were lighted up by the dread god,
  Ares, himself and his armor,
and the shining from his eyes was like fire.
  Who that was only
mortal could have been so hardy
  as to advance upon him
except only Herakles and glorious Iolaos?
75 For the strength of these was great and arms
  and hands irresistible
grew, out of the shoulders of each,
  and their massive bodies.
Now Herakles spoke to his charioteer,
  strong Iolaos:
  "Iolaos, O hero, far dearest to me
  of all mortals,
surely Amphitryon had sinned greatly
  against the blessed
80 immortals who hold Olympos at that time when,
  leaving Tiryns,
the strong-founded citadel, he came to Thebes
  of the ring wall,

after he had killed Elektryon
  over the broad-faced cattle,
and came before Kreon and Enioche
  of the trailing garments,
who greeted him; and gave him all
  that was becoming, as
85 is right to do with suppliants,
  and for this fact their hearts respected him
all the more, and he lived in delight
  with Elektryon's fair-stepping daughter,
his wife; and presently, in the turning
  of the seasons, we two
were born, your father and I,
  though we were not alike either
in body's growth or mind; for Zeus
  took away the wits of Iphikles,
90 and he went away, and forsook his own house
  and his own parents,
and went to pay court to the man
  of evil ways, Eurystheus;
harsh man; and in truth, afterwards,
  he much regretted it
and grieved for his folly, but what was done
  could not be recovered.
But for my share, the spirit has loaded
  hard trials upon me.
95 So, dear friend, make haste:
  you hold the crimsoned reins
of the fast-footed horses, and raising
  in your heart valor to greatness
hold straight ahead the swift chariot
  and the strength of the fast-footed

horses, nor fear the crashing
  of manslaughtering Ares
who now, screaming aloud,
  courses all over the sacred
100 grove of Phoibos Apollo,
    the lord of far-ranging arrows.
Strong though Ares is, this passion
  for battle is madness."
    In turn again, Iolaos the handsome
  spoke to him:
"My uncle, in very fact the father
  of gods and mortals
exalts your head, as does the bull-god,
  the Shaker of the Earth
105 who keeps the coronal of Thebes,
  and defends the high city,
for such is even this man, one tall
  and powerful, whom
he leads in your hand's reach,
  so you can win high glory.
But come, put on your armor of battle,
  so that, with all speed,
we may bring together the two chariots,
  ours and Ares',
110 and fight; he will not terrify
  either yourself, the fearless
son of Zeus, nor me, Iphikles' son; no,
  I think rather
he must run away before the two children
  of blameless Alkeides
who now are close upon him and longing
  to begin the clamor

of battle, which to them is far dearer
  than any festival."
115   So he spoke, and Herakles in his strength
  smiled on him
joyful at heart, for Iolaos spoke
  as he would have wished him to,
and he spoke in turn, answering,
  and addressed him in winged words:
"Iolaos, O hero, illustrious,
  the rough encounter
is not far off now, so, with that skill
  you have always
120 had, now guide the great horse,
  Arion of the black mane,
through all his turns and make him help us,
  as best you are able."
  So speaking, Herakles fastened over
  his shins greaves
of shining tempered bronze,
  the glorious gifts of Hephaistos,
and next about both sides of his chest
  he put on the corselet
125 which was handsome, and gold,
  and much inwrought, and once was given him
by Pallas Athene, daughter of Zeus,
  on that time when first
he was about to launch himself
  on his sorrowful labors;
and now about his shoulders the dreaded man
  put the iron
guard against blows, and looped to his chest
  and hanging backward

130 slung on the hollow quiver,
    with many arrows inside it;
stiffening things, bestowers of death
    and the forgetting of voices;
and they held death at the front end of them,
    and drizzled tears,
but the middle parts were smooth,
    and very long, and the back ends
hidden beneath the feathers
    taken from a golden eagle.
135 Then he took up a ponderous spear,
    headed with shining bronze,
and over his powerful head
    he set the strong-fashioned helmet
intricately wrought of steel,
    and it fitted over
his temples, and this guarded the head
    of godlike Herakles.
    In his hands he took up his shield,
    all-glancing, nor could anyone
140 break it, either by cast or stroke,
    a wonder to look at.
For all about the circle of it,
    with enamel and with pale
ivory, and with electrum it shone,
    and with gold glowing
it was bright, and there were folds
    of cobalt driven upon it.
In the middle was a face of Panic,
    not to be spoken of,
145 glaring on the beholder
    with eyes full of fire glinting,

and the mouth of it was full of teeth,
  terrible, repugnant
and glittering white, while over
  the lowering forehead hovered
a figure of dread Hate, marshaling
  the slaughter of fighting men,
cruel spirit, who took the senses
  and perception out of

150 those fighters who tried to fight
  in the face of Zeus' son, the War God,
and the souls of these went under the ground,
  to the house of Hades,
and lay there, while the bones,
  with the dry skin rotting upon them,
festered along the black earth
  under the Sun-star's withering.
    On it were wrought the figures of Onrush
  and Backrush, on it

155 Battlenoise and Panic
  and Manslaughter were blazing,
and Hate was there with Confusion among them,
  and Death the destructive;
she was holding a live man with a new wound,
  and another
one unhurt, and dragged a dead man
  by the feet through the carnage.
The clothing upon her shoulders
  showed strong red with the men's blood,

160 as she glared, horribly,
  and gnashed her teeth till they echoed.
    And on it were the heads of snakes,
  dreaded, indescribable,

twelve of them, who across the land
  pursued the races of mortals,
those fighters who tried to fight
  in the face of Zeus's son, Herakles.
And when Amphitryon's son did battle,
  the sound of the grinding
165 of their teeth came out,
    and these wonderful works of art blazed up,
and it looked as if the mottled marking
  of these terrible great snakes
could be seen, bluish upon the backs,
  but at the jaws darkening.
    And on it there were masses of wild pigs,
  and of lions
glaring against each other, full of rage,
  straining to advance,
170 and the ranks of them were ranged
  in companies, nor could you see
either side flinch from the other.
  Both bristled their backs up, and now
already there was lying between them
  one great lion, and by him
two wild boars, the life gone out of them,
  and the black blood
running off them into the ground, as they,
  with necks extended
175 lay there, fallen to the assault
  of the grim-faced lions;
but for this, both sides were only
  all the more stirred up, raging
to do battle, alike the wild pigs
  and the glare-eyed lions.

And on it was the battle
of the Lapith spearmen, fighting
about the Lord Kaineus, and Dryas
and Peirithoös,
180   Hopleus and Exadios,
and Prolochos and Phaleros,
and Mopsos son of Ampyke, from Titaresia,
scion of Ares,
and Theseus, Aigeus' son,
in the likeness of the immortals.
These were in silver, but upon their bodies
they wore armor
of gold; and over against them, facing,
were gathered the Centaurs
185   fighting about great Petraios,
and Asbolos the diviner,
Arktos and Oureios,
and Mimas of the black hair,
and the two sons of Peukeus, Dryalos
and Perimedes,
and these were in silver, but the fir trees
they had in their hands
were golden, and they were streaming together,
as if they were alive,
190   and battering each other in close combat
with spears and fir trunks.
    And on it were standing
the swift-footed horses of grim-faced
Ares, in gold, and he himself, the spoiler,
the destructive,
gripping his spear in his hands
and calling out to the foot-fighters,

and stained red with blood,
 as if he stood in his chariot
195 and were killing real, live men,
  and beside him Terror and Panic
stood, straining forward
 to get into the battle of warriors.
  And on it was Zeus' daughter,
Athene Tritogeneia
the spoiler, like herself when she wishes
 to marshal the battle,
holding in her hands the spear
 and wearing the golden helmet
200 with the aegis upon her shoulders,
  and she was entering the dread battle.
  And on it was the sacred chorale
of the immortals,
in whose midst the son of Zeus
 and Leto made lovely
205 music on his golden lyre,
  and the Muses of Pieria,
goddesses, led the chorus in the likeness
 of clear singers.
  And on it was an anchorage
of the restless sea, good harbor,
wrought upon a circle of pure tin,
 and it was made
like rough water, and out on the surface
 of it were many
210 dolphins, fishing, and plunging
 about one way and another
as if they were swimming,
 and two in particular, done in silver,

were blowing, as they darted
  after the scaly fishes,
and the fish, done in bronze,
  fled away before them; meanwhile, on the rocks,
a fisherman was sitting, waiting his chance,
  and holding
215 a fishing net in his hands, made like one
  who was about to cast it.
    And on it was made Perseus, the rider,
  the son of fair-tressed
Danaë, who did not touch the shield
  with his feet, but they were not
far, a great wonder to try to describe,
  for they were not supported,
this being handicraft from the renowned smith
  of the strong arms
220 done in gold. On Perseus' feet
  were the flying sandals,
and across his shoulders was slung
  the black-bound sword, suspended
on a sword-belt of bronze, and he hovered
  like a thought in the mind,
and all his back was covered
  with the head of the monster, the dreaded
Gorgon, and the bag floated about it,
  a wonder to look at,
225 done in silver, but the shining tassels
  fluttered, and they
were gold, and the temples
  of the lord Perseus were hooded over
by the war-cap of Hades, which confers
  terrible darkness.

The son of Danaë, Perseus himself,
  sped onward, like one who
goes in haste and terror, as meanwhile
  the rest of the Gorgons
230 tumbled along behind him, unapproachable,
    indescribable,
straining to catch and grab him,
  and on the green of the steel
surface gibbered the sound of their feet
  on the shield running
with a sharp high noise,
  and on the belts of the Gorgons a pair
of snakes were suspended,
  but they reared and bent their heads forward
235 and flickered with their tongues.
    The teeth for their rage were made jagged
and their staring fierce,
  and over the dreaded heads of the Gorgons
was great Panic shivering.
                  On the space of
  the shield above these
were men, with the warlike armor upon them,
  fighting in battle,
some striving to beat destruction away
  from their own city
240 and their own parents, while the others
  were raging to sack the city.
Many men were down, but more yet
  were still fighting
and in combat, while on their
  strong-built bastions, which were done
in bronze, their women cried sharp
  and shrill, tore their cheeks

with their nails, like living women:
  the work of glorious Hephaistos.
245 And men, the seniors, on whom old age
  had seized already,
were sitting assembled outside the gates,
  and holding up their hands
to the immortal gods, being in fear
  for the sake of their children,
and these for their part were fighting
  their battle, and where they were
the Spirits of Death, dark-colored,
  and clattering their white teeth,
250 deadly-faced, grim-glaring, bloody
  and unapproachable,
were fighting over the fallen men,
  all of them rushing forward
to drink of the black blood; and each,
  as soon as she had snatched
a man, down already, or just dropping
  from a wound, would hook her great claws
about his body, while his soul went down
  to the realm of Hades
255 and cold Tartaros. Then when the Spirits
  had sated their senses
on the blood of men's slaughter,
  they would throw what was left behind them
and go storming back into the battle-clamor
  and the struggle.
Klotho and Lachesis stood over them,
  and smaller
than they was Atropos, no tall goddess,
  yet she it is

260 who is eldest of them,
  and ranked high beyond the two others.
  And all of these were making
   a grisly fight over
  one man, glaring horribly at each other
   with eyes full of anger
  and making an equal fight of it
   with claws and bold hands,
  and beside them was standing Deathmist,
   dismal and dejected,
265 green and pale, dirty-dry,
   fallen in on herself with hunger,
  knee-swollen, and the nails were grown long
   on her hands, and from
  her nostrils the drip kept running,
   and off her cheeks
  the blood dribbled to the ground,
   and she stood there, grinning
270 forever, and the dust that had gathered
   and lay in heaps on her shoulders
  was muddy with tears.
                    Next this was a city
   of men, well walled,
  and golden were the seven gates
   that were in it, fitted
  with lintels, and the people in it,
   with merrymaking and dances,
  held festival, for some,
   in a smooth-running mule-carriage,
  were bringing the bride to the groom,
   and the loud bride-song was arising.
275 Far away there flared the light
   of the torches blazing

in the hands of the serving-maids, and they,
  festive in the occasion,
ran on ahead, and the choruses
  came after them, playing;
the men, to the accompaniment of clear pipes,
  were singing
from their light mouths, and the sound
  of their voices was breaking about them,
280 while the girls, to the music of lyres,
  led on the lovely chorus.
There again, on the other side,
  young men reveled to the music
of the flute, some playing to it
  with dancing and singing,
while others, each in time
  to the flute player, and laughing,
ran on ahead, and the whole city
  was in the hold of festivity
285 and dancing and delight.

                  Now there were others,
  in front of the city,
mounted astride horses, and galloping,
  and there were plowmen
breaking up the divine earth,
  and made with their tunics
tucked up. Now the soil of the land
  was deep, and some, with sharpened
sickles, were reaping the down-curving heads,
  that weighted
290 the stalks, as if they were harvesting
  the yield of Demeter,
and some were sheaving them in binders,
  and strewing the threshing floor,

and some, with reaping hooks in their hands,
  were cutting the grapes, while
others again took from the gatherers
  and put in baskets
the grape clusters, black and white,
  from the great vine-rows
295 which were weighted down by their foliage
  and silvery tendrils,
while others again carried the baskets,
  and next them the vine-row
was done in gold, the glorious work
  of careful Hephaistos,
shivering with leaves, and with vine-poles
  done in silver, and weighted
300 down beneath its clusters, and these again
  had been darkened.
Some were treading, others draining
  the juice, while others were contending
in matches, with fists, or wrestling,
  while others again, who were huntsmen,
were chasing fleet-footed hares
  with their rip-fanged dogs in front of them,
racing to catch the hares who raced
  to get away from them.
305   Next to them, there were horsemen toiling,
  who for the sake
of a prize contended and labored,
  and the charioteers, standing
in the strong-fabricated chariots,
  raced their fast horses
with reins slackened,
  and the compacted chariots, thundering

along, flew swift, with the axles
  in the naves screaming.
310 So they toiled on, unendingly,
  nor ever had victory
been won by any of them, but their race
  was yet undecided;
and before them, in the infield,
  was set as a prize a great tripod
done in gold, the glorious work
  of careful Hephaistos.
    And about the shield rim ran the stream
  of the Ocean, looking
315 like flood tide, and held together
  all the elaborate shield, and upon it
swans, some soaring and singing a high song,
  while many others
swam on the water surface where fish
  swarmed away before them.

It was a wonder to look at,
  even for Zeus deep-thundering, through
whose counsels Hephaistos
  had made the shield, great and massive,
320 fitting it with his hands.
                   And now the powerful
  son of Zeus
swung it with full control and leaped down
  from the horse-chariot
like a lightning-flash from the hand
  of his father, Zeus of the aegis,
stepping light on his feet,
  and his charioteer, strong Iolaos,

standing firm on its floor steered
  the curved chariot. Meanwhile,
325 the goddess, Athene of the gray eyes,
  came and stood close beside them
and spoke to them in encouragement
  and addressed them in winged words:
    "Hail, generation of Lynkeus famed afar.
  Now
Zeus, lord over the immortals,
  grants you the triumph,
to kill Kyknos, and to strip away
  his glorious armor.
330 But another thing I will say to you now,
  O best of all people.
After you have robbed Kyknos
  of the sweetness of life, then
you must leave him where he is,
  and his armor with him,
and yourself keep your eye
  on manslaughtering Ares, as he
advances, and where, watching,
  you see a bare place, under
335 the elaborate shield, there stab him
  with the sharp bronze, then
draw back and away; it has not been destined
  for you to capture
either the horses of Kyknos,
  or his glorious armor."
    So she spoke, shining among goddesses,
  and mounted the chariot
swiftly, holding in her immortal hands
  victory, and the glory

340 of success; and then Iolaos,
      descended of heaven, cried out
   a terrible cry to his horses, and they,
      to their master's outcry,
   lightly and dustily through the plain
      pulled the fast chariot.
   For in them, with a flourish of her aegis,
      the goddess
   gray-eyed Athene inspired courage,
      and the earth thundered
345 about them, and the others came on opposed,
      like fire, like a stormcloud,
   Kyknos breaker of horses
      and Ares insatiate of battle,
   and as their horses on either side
      came facing, they neighed
   sharply, and the sound of their voices
      was breaking about them.
   First of the two heroes to speak
      was the mighty Herakles:
350 "Kyknos, old friend, why do you hold
      your fast horses against us
   now? We are men well versed in the toil
      and sorrow of battle.
   No, now, hold to one side
      your polished chariot, and let us
   go through on the road. I will tell you.
      I am passing through to Trachis
   and the lord Keÿx, who is pre-eminent in Trachis, for power
355 and respect in which he is held,
      and you yourself know him well,
   seeing you are married to his daughter,
      dark-eyed Themistonoë.

Ares, old friend, will not be able
  to keep the ending of death
from you, if ever we once come together
  in combat. Even
before now, I claim, he has at one time
  had experience
360 of my spear, upon that time when,
    above sandy Pylos,
he stood up against me, raging hard
  in fury for battle,
and three times, under the stabbing
  of my spear on his shield, he was
knocked down upon the ground,
  and the fourth time, I thrust
with all my rage at his thigh
  and split a great hole in his body,
365 and headlong into the dust he tumbled then,
    under my spearing.
And there he might have been disgraced
  among the gods, if
he had gone down under my hands
  and left the bloody spoils to me."
  So he spoke, but Kyknos
  of the strong ash spear did not
at all ponder obeying
  and checking the horses that drew
370 his chariot. Now both leapt suddenly
    to the ground from strong-fabricated
chariots: the son of Zeus
  and the son of the Lord of Battles.
The charioteers drove
  their fluttering-maned horses close

together, and under their hastening feet
  the broad earth thundered.
As when, from the towering pinnacle
  of a great mountain,
375 boulders spring off and come down,
  tumbling one against another,
and many oaks with sweeping foliage,
  many pines
and black poplars that spread wide
  their roots are splintered beneath them
as they roll and nimbly bounce
  until they come to the flat land;
so these two, screaming high,
  crashed together, and all
380 the city of the Myrmidons, and famous Iolkos,
Arne and Helike and Antheia of the grasses,
re-echoed to the sound of their battlecries,
  and they with inhuman
clamor came on, and Zeus of the counsels
  crashed a great stroke
and he wept tears of blood that rained
  from the sky, to make
385 memorable his high-hearted son's
  battle-encounter.
    As, in the ravines of the mountains,
  a toothy boar, hard
to track down, is minded in his heart
  to fight it out
against the men who are hunting him, and,
  at bay turning,
sharpens his white teeth,
  and the slaver dribbles at his mouth

390   as he grinds them together,
   and his eyes are like fire blazing,
  and on his spine and the back of his neck
   the bristles stiffen up;
  such was the son of Zeus as he sprang
   from his horse-drawn chariot.
  And at the time when the dark-winged
   loud grasshopper, sitting
  on a green branch, begins to sing
   in the summer for mortal
395   people; his food and drink
   are the female dew; and starting
  with the dawn, and all day long,
   he pours his voice out, in
  the time of the most terrible heat,
   when the Sun-star burns skin;
  at which time the grain-heads ripen
   upon the millet
  that men sow in summer,
   when the grapes bunch up into clusters,
400   what Dionysos has given to men,
   a joy and a burden;
  this season the heroes fought,
   and a great tumult rose up;
  as of two lions who, over the body
   of a killed deer,
  rage against each other and charge,
   and terrible
  is the crying that goes up
   and the noise of their teeth snapping;
405   and they, then, as two hook-clawed,
   beak-bent vultures

above a tall rock-face
  high-screaming go for each other
over a goat that ranges the mountains,
  or a fat deer
of the wilds; some young hunter
  has made a shot, and killed it
with an arrow from his bowstring,
  but he has gone straying elsewhere
410 not knowing the ground, and the vultures
  have been quick to perceive it
and have swooped down
  and begun a grim battle over him;
so now these two heroes, screaming,
  went for each other.
    And now Kyknos, furious to kill the son
  of powerful
Zeus, made a cast into the shield
  with his brazen spear,
415 but could not break the bronze,
  and the gift of the god guarded him.
And now Amphitryon's son,
  Herakles the powerful, swiftly
struck, and forcibly with the long spear,
  between helm
and shield, where the throat
  had been left unguarded, beneath
the chin, and the manslaughtering ash spear
  cut through
420 both tendons, for great was the strength
  of the man that was driven behind it.
He fell, then, as some oak goes down,
  or a sky-towering

pine tree, stricken by the smoky thunderbolt
of Zeus. So
he fell, and his armor elaborate
  with bronze clashed upon him.
    Then the stout-hearted son of Zeus
left him to lie there
425 and himself kept watch
  on manslaughtering Ares, as he came onward,
keeping his dread eyes upon him,
  like a lion that has come on
a victim, and, with his strong claws,
  violently tears up
the hide, and with no time lost
  robs the victim of sweet life;
and the heart of him is filled
  and darkened within by anger,
430 and with terrible green glare in his eyes,
  with his tail he lashes
his own ribs and shoulders,
  and digs with his claws, and no one
who watches him has the courage to go close
  or fight against him;
such was the son of Amphitryon,
  insatiate of battle,
as he stood up to face Ares,
  advancing on him and swelling
435 the valor within; and the other
  came close to him, heart vexed with fury,
and the two of them, screaming aloud,
  advanced to encounter.
As when a boulder, breaking loose,
  springs from a great cliff
and rolls down in long bounces, and with furious force

and crashing noise goes on, but then
  there is a high cliff standing
440 in its way, and the boulder crashes into it,
  and is stopped there;
with such tumult Ares the destructive,
  burden of chariots,
charged crying aloud on Herakles,
  who came eagerly to meet him.
    But now Athene, daughter of Zeus
  of the aegis, came
to stand in the path of Ares,
  herself wearing the gloomy aegis.
445 She looked scowling terribly at him
  and spoke in winged words:
"Ares, stay now your fury and power,
  and your hands invincible;
for you are not permitted to kill Herakles,
  the bold-hearted
son of Zeus, and then despoil
  him of his glorious armor;
so come, stop this battle,
  and do not stand up against me."
450   So she spoke, but could not persuade
  the great heart in Ares,
but he, screaming aloud,
  flourishing his spear like a flame,
rapidly made his rush
  against the powerful Herakles,
furious to kill him, and cast at him
  with the bronze spear
in anger and resentment
  for his son who was fallen,

455   and struck the great shield,
    but gray-eyed Athene, reaching
out of the chariot, turned aside
  the shock of the spearhead.
The bitter sorrow closed on Ares,
  and drawing his sharp sword
he swept in against Herakles
  the strong-hearted, but as he came in
Amphitryon's son, insatiate
  of the terrible battle-cry,
460   stabbed with full force
    into the thigh left bare under
the elaborate shield, and twisting
  with the spear tore
a great hole in the flesh,
  and beat him to the ground between.
Then Panic and Terror drove
  their smooth-running chariot and horses
close up to him, and lifted him
  from the wide-wayed earth
465   and set him in the elaborate chariot,
    and presently
lashed on the horses,
  and they made their way to tall Olympos.
    But Herakles, son of Alkmene,
  with glorious Iolaos,
stripped the splendid armor
  from the shoulders of Kyknos
and hastened on, and presently
  with their fast-footed horses
470   reached the citadel of Trachis,
    while gray-eyed Athene

made her way to great Olympos
  and the house of her father.
    But Kyknos was buried by Keÿx
  and the numberless people
of that glorious King, those who lived
  in the cities thereabouts,
in Anthe, the city of the Myrmidons,
  and famous Iolkos,
475 Arne and Helike, and a great multitude
  was assembled
doing honor to Keÿx who was the friend
  of the blessed immortals.
But the river Anauros, swollen
  with winter rain, obliterated
the barrow and the grave;
  for this was the will of Leto's
son, Apollo; because Kyknos had waylaid
  and forcibly
robbed the glorious hecatombs,
  as men brought them to Pytho.

Genealogical Tables

A THE ORIGINAL GODS

Chaos   Gaia   Tartaros   Eros

Note: Although Chaos came first (T 116) it is not stated that Chaos begot the other original gods.

B

Chaos *(no consort mentioned)*

Erebos = Night

Aither   Hemera

C

Gaia *(without consort)*

Ourea   Pontos

Ouranos

D

Gaia = Tartaros

Typhoeus

E THE GREAT GENERATION OF TITANS

(A) Gaia = Ouranos (C)

Okeanos Koios Krios Hyperion Iapetos Theia Rheia Themis Mnemosyne Phoibe Tethys Kronos Brontes Steropes Arges Kottos Briareos Gyes

F

(A) Gaia = the blood of Ouranos

Furies   Giants   Nymphs of the Ash Trees

G

Members of Ouranos

Aphrodite

H THE CHILDREN OF NIGHT

(B) Night (without consort)

Moros | Thanatos | Oneiroi | Oizys | Moirai | Nemesis | Philotes | Eris
Ker | Hypnos | Momos | Hesperides | Keres | Apate | Geras

I (H) Eris (no consort mentioned)

Ponos | Limos | Hysminai | Phonoi | Neikea | Amphilogiai | Ate
Lethe | Algea | Machai | Androktasiai | Logoi | Dysnomia | Horkos

J

(A) Gaia = Ouranos (C)   (C) Pontos = Gaia (A)

Okeanos = Tethys

Doris = Nereus   Thaumas   Phorkys = Keto   Eurybia

Nereids   Graiai   Gorgons

The Snake at the World's End

K

(C) Pontos = (A) Gaia = Ouranos (C)

Okeanos = Tethys

Thaumas = Elektra

Iris   Harpies

L

Blood of Medusa   (E) Okeanos = Tethys (E)

Chrysaör = Kallirhoë   Echidna = Typhaön

Geryon   Orthos   Kerberos   Hydra
                                            Chimaira

M

(L) Echidna = Orthos (L)

  Sphinx   Nemeian Lion

N

(E) Okeanos = Tethys (E)

  Rivers   Okeanids

O

(A) Gaia = Ouranos (C)

(E) Theia = Hyperion (E)

  Helios   Selene   Eos

P

(J) Eurybia = Krios (E)   (E) Phoibe = Koios (E)   (E) Kronos = Rheia (E)

(O) Eos = Astraios   Pallas = Styx, an Okeanid (N)   Perses = Asteria   Leto = Zeus

Zephyros Boreas Notos   Eosphoros Stars   Hekate   Apollo Artemis

    Zelos Nike Kratos Bia

Q THE GREAT GENERATION OF OLYMPIANS

(A) Gaia = Ouranos (C)

(E) Rheia = Kronos (E)

Histia Demeter = Zeus = Hera Hades Poseidon

  Persephone Ares Hebe Eileithyia

R

(E) Okeanos = Tethys (E)

(E) Iapetos = Klymene, an Okeanid (N)

Atlas | Prometheus | Epimetheus | Menoitios

(Q) Zeus = Maia
    Hermes

S

(Q) Zeus = Metis, an Okeanid (N)
    Athene

T

(Q) Zeus = Themis (E)

Horai | Fates

(Eunomia, Dike, Eirene)   (Klotho, Lachesis, Atropos)

U

(Q) Zeus = Eurynome, an Okeanid (N)
    Graces

V

(Q) Zeus = Mnemosyne (E)
    Muses

W

(Q) Poseidon = Amphitrite, a Nereïd (J)
Triton

(Q) Hera (*without consort*)
Hephaistos = Aglaia, one of the Graces (U)

(Q) Zeus = Alkmene, a mortal
Herakles = Hebe (Q)

(G) Aphrodite = Ares (Q)
Panic   Terror   Harmonia = Kadmos, a mortal
Semele = Zeus (Q)
Dionysos = Ariadne

Glossary

This glossary is not a complete index. Casual references have generally not been noted. Particular attention has been given to the notice of birth in the *Theogony*. Place names have been omitted. (Rivers are treated as persons.)

In the names of certain gods, the translator is faced with a difficulty. All names originally mean something, but in what might be called the pure name, the form of the meaningful term has been modified, the elementary meaning is obscure or disputed, and one merely transliterates the name: e. g., Zeus, Kronos, Poseidon. At the other extreme are the names of gods which are also simply common nouns standing for qualities, activities, situations: e. g., Dike is Justice, the Hysminai are Battles, etc. It has generally seemed better to translate these terms in the text, so as to show the interrelation of concepts in Hesiod. In such cases, both the Greek name and its translation have usually been listed in the glossary. Justice, for instance, will be found under both Justice and Dike. Greek names are mostly used in the genealogies.

The Greek and English terms do not, however, always have a one-to-one equivalence. Rendering may have to vary according to context. Thus for Eris no single term seems to fit. In *The Works and Days* (11) I have called her "Strife," but in *Theogony* I have gone to the conventional translation, "Discord." I am not sure, in view of her children, that here "Disorder" might not be better; one of her children is, for instance, Lethe, who is not only Forgetfulness, but also Indifference or Unawareness; but the line has to be drawn somewhere.

A guide to syllabic stress is given. There is no silent final *e* in Greek, and such a name as Hebe will always be two syllables, not one.

I have avoided the Latinized forms, as I did in my translation of *The Iliad*, except for a few familiar names like Jason, Circe, Apollo.

Abbreviations are s (*Shield of Herakles*), T (*Theogony*), and w (*Works and Days*).

Acheloi′os: a River. T340.
Achil′leus: son of Peleus and Thetis. T1007.
Achlys: Deathmist, a Spirit. s264.
Adme′te: an Okeanid. T349.
Aël′lo: a Harpy. T267.
Affection (Philotes): child of Night. T224.
Agau′e: a Nereïd. T247.
Agau′e: daughter of Kadmos and Harmonia. T976.
Aglai′a: one of the Graces. T909; 946.
Ag′rios: son of Odysseus and Circe. T1013.
Ai′akos: husband of Psamathe. T1004.
Aïdo′neus: by-name of Hades. T913.
Aidos: Respect or Shame, a Spirit. w197; 317.
Aie′tes: son of Helios and Perseïs. T957.
Aig′eus: father of Theseus. s182.
Ainei′as: son of Anchises and Aphrodite. T1009.
Aise′pos: a River. T342.
Aison: father of Jason. T992.
Aither: the bright Air, child of Night and Erebos. T124.
Akas′te: an Okeanid. T356.
Aktai′ë: a Nereïd. T249.
Al′gea, the: the Pains, children of Discord. T227.

Alkai'os: father of Amphitryon. s26.
Alkme'ne: wife of Amphitryon, mother of Herakles. T943; s3.
Alphei'os: a River. T338.
Amphi'damas: baron at Chalkis. w655.
Amphilo'giai, the: the Disputations, children of Discord. T229.
Am'phiro: an Okeanid. T360.
Amphi'trite: a Nereïd. T243; 252; 930.
Amphi'tryon: husband of Alkmene. s2; 79. Called Alkeides, "son of Alkaios," s112.
Am'pyke: mother of Mopsos. s181.
Anchi'ses: husband of Aphrodite. T1009.
Androkta'siai, the: the Manslaughters, children of Discord. T228. In singular, s155.
A'pate: Deception, daughter of Night. T224.
Aphrodi'te: also called Kytherei'a, Philomme'dea, Kyprogenei'a, born from the members of Ouranos. T200; 933; 1008; w65.
Apollo: son of Zeus and Leto. T919; w771; s58; 479.
Ardes'kos: a River. T345.
Ares: son of Zeus and Hera. T923; 934; s57; 109; 192; 357; 425.
Ar'ges: one of the Kyklopes. T140.
Ariad'ne: daughter of Minos, wife of Dionysos. T947.
A'rimoi: a people of the north. T304.
Ari'on: chariot horse of Iolaos. s120.
Aristai'os: husband of Autonoë. T977.
Arktos: a Centaur. s186.
Ar'temis: daughter of Zeus and Leto. T919.
As'bolos: a Centaur. s185.
Asia: an Okeanid. T359.
Aste'ria: daughter of Koios and Phoibe. T409.
Astrai'os: son of Krios and Eurybia. T367; 379.
Ate: Ruin, daughter of Discord. T230.
Athe'ne: daughter of Zeus and Metis. T889; 929a; of Zeus alone, T924; see also w63; s126; 325; 443.
Atlas: son of Iapetos and Klymene. T509; 517; 746.

A'tropos: one of the Fates. T218; 905; S254.
Auto'noë: a Nereïd. T258.
Auto'noë: daughter of Kadmos and Harmonia. T977.

Backrush (Palioxis): a Spirit. S154.
Battlenoise (Homados): a Spirit. S155.
Battles, the (Hysminai): children of Discord. T228.
Belle'rophon (Bellerophon'tes): killer of Chimaira. T325.
Bia: Force, daughter of Pallas and Styx. T385.
Bo'reas: the (north) Wind, son of Astraios and Eos. T380;
    870; W505.
Bri'areos: also called Obriareos, son of Ouranos and Gaia.
    T149; 617; 734.
Brontes: one of the Kyklopes. T140.

Centaurs, the: enemies of the Lapithai. S184.
Chaos: the first of the Gods. T116.
Cha'rites, the: the Graces, daughters of Zeus and Eury-
    nome. T908.
Cheiron: teacher of Medeios. T1001.
Chimai'ra: beast, daughter of Hydra. T319; 325.
Chry'saör: born of Medusa's blood. T281; 288; 980.
Chryse'ïs: an Okeanid. T359.
Circe (Kirke): daughter of Helios and Perseïs. T957; 1011.
Confusion (Kydoimos): a Spirit. S156.

Da'naë: mother of Perseus. S217.
Day (Hemera): child of Night and Erebos. T124; 748.
Death (Thanatos): son of Night. T212; 759.
Deathmist (Achlys): a Spirit. S264.
Deception (Apate): daughter of Night. T224.
Deimos: Terror, son of Ares and Aphrodite. T934; S463.
Deme'ter: daughter of Kronos and Rheia. T454; 912; 969;
    W200; 465.
Destinies, the (Moirai): daughters of Night. T217.
Dike: Justice, one of the Seasons. T902; W217; 256.
Dio'ne: an Okeanid. T353.
Diony'sos: son of Zeus and Semele. T941; 947.

Discord (Eris): child of Night. T225.

Disputations, the (Amphilogiai): children of Discord. T229.

Doris: an Okeanid, wife of Nereus, mother of the Nereïds. T240; 350.

Doris: a Nereïd. T250.

Dos: Give, a Spirit. w356.

Doto: a Nereïd. T248.

Dreams, the (Oneiroi): children of Night. T212.

Dry'alos: a Centaur. s187.

Dryas: a Lapith. s179.

Dyna'mene: a Nereïd. T248.

Dysno'mia: Lawlessness, daughter of Discord: T230.

Echid'na: daughter of Kallirhoë. T297; 326.

Eileithy'ia: daughter of Zeus and Hera. T923.

Eï'one: a Nereïd. T255.

Eire'ne: Peacetime, one of the Seasons. T902; w228.

Elek'tra: an Okeanid, wife of Thaumas. T265; 349.

Elek'tryon: father of Alkmene. s3; 82.

Elpis: Hope, a Spirit. w96.

Ema'thion: a son of Tithonos and Eos. T985.

Eni'oche: wife of Kreon. s83.

En'yo: one of the Graiai. T273.

Eos: Dawn, daughter of Hyperion and Theia. T372; 378; 984.

Eos'phoros: the Dawnstar, son of Astraios and Eos. T381.

Epime'theus: son of Iapetos and Klymene. T511; w85.

E'rato: one of the Muses. T78.

E'rato: a Nereïd. T246.

E'rebos: Darkness, child of Chaos. T123.

Eri'danos: a River. T338.

Erigenei'a: by-name of Eos ("early-born"). T381.

Erin'yes, the: the Furies, born of the blood of Ouranos. T185; w803.

Eris: Discord, child of Night. In *Works and Days* and *The Shield*, translated Strife. T225; w11; 804; s148; 156.

Eros: Love, an original god. T120; 201.
Eua'gore: a Nereïd. T257.
Euar'ne: a Nereïd. T259.
Eudo'ra: a Nereïd. T244.
Eudo'ra: an Okeanid. T360.
Eue'nos: a River. T345.
Eukran'te: a Nereïd. T243.
Euli'mene: a Nereïd. T247.
Euni'ke: a Nereïd. T246.
Euno'mia: Lawfulness, one of the Seasons. T902.
Euphro'syne: one of the Graces. T909.
Eupom'pe: a Nereïd. T261.
Euro'pa: an Okeanid. T357.
Eury'ale: a Gorgon. T276.
Eury'bia: daughter of Pontos. T239; 375.
Eury'nome: an Okeanid. T358; 907.
Eurys'theus: taskmaster of Herakles. s89.
Eury'tion: oxherd of Geryon. T293.
Euter'pe: one of the Muses. T77.
Exa'dios: a Lapith. s180.

Fates, the (Moirai or perhaps Keres): daughters of Night.
    T217; daughters of Zeus and Themis, T904.
Force (Bia): daughter of Pallas and Styx. T385.
Forgetfulness (Lethe): daughter of Discord. T227.
Furies, the (Erinyes): born from the blood of Ouranos.
    T185; w803.

Gaia: Earth, an original god. T106; 117; 238; 607; 821.
Galatei'a: a Nereïd. T250.
Galaxau'ra: an Okeanid. T353.
Gale'ne: a Nereïd. T244.
Geras: Old Age, child of Night. T225.
Ge'ryon (Gery'ones): son of Chrysaör and Kallirhoë.
    T289; 982.
Giants, the: born from the blood of Ouranos. T185.
Give (Dos): a Spirit. w356.
Glauke: a Nereïd. T244.

Glauko'nome: a Nereïd. T256.

Gorgons, the: daughters of Phorkys and Keto. T274; S224.

Gossip (Pheme): a Concept raised to the status of Spirit.
   w760.

Grab (Harpax): a Spirit. w356.

Graces, the (Charites): daughters of Zeus and Eurynome.
   T908.

Graiai: the gray sisters, daughters of Phorkys and Keto.
   T270.

Gre'nikos: a River. T342.

Grievances, the (Neikea): children of Discord. T229.

Gyes: son of Ouranos and Gaia. T149; 618; 713; 734.

Hades: son of Kronos and Rheia. T455; 768; 913.

Ha'lia: a Nereïd. T245.

Haliak'mon: a River. T341.

Halime'de: a Nereïd. T255.

Hardship (Ponos): son of Discord. T226.

Harmo'nia: daughter of Ares and Aphrodite. T937; 975.

Harpax: Grab, a Spirit. w356.

Harpies, the: daughters of Thaumas and Elektra. T267.

Hebe: daughter of Zeus and Hera. T923; 953.

He'kate: daughter of Perses and Asteria. T411.

Helen: Queen of Sparta. w165.

Helios: the Sun, son of Hyperion and Theia. T371; 956;
   1011.

He'mera: Day, child of Night and Erebos. T124; 748.

Hephaistos: son of Hera. T928; 945; w60; s123; 319.

Hepta'poros: a River. T341.

Hera: daughter of Kronos and Rheia. T454; 921.

He'rakles: son of Zeus and Alkmene. T289; 318; 527; 944;
   950; s52; 349.

Hermes: son of Zeus and Maia. T939; w67.

Hermos: a River. T343.

Hespe'rides, the: daughters of Night. T215.

Hills, the (Ourea): children of Gaia. T129.

Hi'meros: Desire, a Spirit. T201.

Hippo: an Okeanid. T351.

Hippo′noë: a Nereïd. T251.
Hippo′thoë: a Nereïd. T251.
His′tia: daughter of Kronos and Rheia. T454.
Ho′mados: Battlenoise, a Spirit. S155.
Hope (Elpis): a Spirit. W96.
Hop′leus: a Lapith. S180.
Horai: the Seasons, daughters of Zeus and Themis. T901.
Horkos: Oath, son of Discord. T231; W219; 804.
Hybris: Violence, a Spirit. W217.
Hydra: daughter of Typhaon and Echidna. T313.
Hype′rion: son of Ouranos and Gaia. T134; 371.
Hypnos: Sleep, son of Night. T212; 759.
Hysmi′nai, the: the Battles, children of Discord. T228.

Ianei′ra: an Okeanid. T356.
Ian′the: an Okeanid. T349.
Ia′petos: son of Ouranos and Gaia. T134; 507.
Ia′sion: husband of Demeter. T970.
Idy′ia: an Okeanid. T352; 961.
Ino: daughter of Kadmos and Harmonia. T976.
Iola′os: son of Iphikles, companion-in-arms of Herakles.
    T318; S74.
I′phikles: son of Amphitryon and Alkmene. S54; 89.
Iris: daughter of Thaumas and Elcktra. T266.
Istros: the Danube, a River. T339.

Jason (Iason): husband of Medeia. T992.
Justice (Dike): one of the Seasons. T902; W217; 256.

Kadmos: husband of Harmonia. T937; 975.
Kaï′kos: a River. T343.
Kai′neus: a Lapith. S179.
Kalli′ope: one of the Muses. T79.
Kalli′rhoë: an Okeanid. T287; 351; 979.
Kalyp′so: an Okeanid. T359; 1017.
Ke′phalos: husband of Eos. T986.

Ker: Fate (of a person), daughter of Night. T211. In plural, possibly the same as Moirai, T218; see also (as Death) s156; 249.

Ker'beros: dog, son of Typhaön and Echidna. T311; 769.

Kerke'is: an Okeanid. T355.

Keto: daughter of Pontos. T238; 270; 333.

Keÿx: king of Trachis. s354; 472.

Kleio: one of the Muses. T77.

Klotho: one of the Fates. T218; 905; s258.

Kly'mene: an Okeanid. T351; 507.

Kly'tia: an Okeanid. T352.

Koios: son of Ouranos and Gaia. T134; 404.

Kottos: son of Ouranos and Gaia. T149; 618; 713; 734.

Kratos: Power, child of Pallas and Styx. T385.

Kreon: king of Thebes. s83.

Krios: son of Ouranos and Gaia. T134; 376.

Kronos: son of Ouranos and Gaia. T137; 168; 453; 460; w111; 169.

Kydoi'mos: Confusion, a Spirit. s156.

Kyklo'pes, the: the Cyclopses, sons of Ouranos and Gaia. T139.

Kyknos: son of Ares. s57; 349; 413.

Kymato'lege: a Nereïd. T252.

Kymo: a Nereïd. T255.

Kymo'doke: a Nereïd. T252.

Kymo'thoë: a Nereïd. T245.

La'chesis: one of the Fates. T218; 905; s258.

Ladon: a River. T344.

Laomedei'a: a Nereïd. T257.

Lapith (ai): the people of Peirithoös. s178.

Lati'nos: son of Odysseus and Circe. T1013.

Lawfulness (Eunomia): one of the Seasons. T902.

Lawlessness (Dysnomia): daughter of Discord. T230.

Lea'gore: a Nereïd. T257.

Lethe: Forgetfulness, daughter of Discord. T227.

Leto: daughter of Koios and Phoibe. T406; 918; w771.

Limos: Starvation, son of Discord. T227; w299.

Logoi, the: the Stories, children of Discord. T229.
Lyn'keus: ancestor of Herakles. S327.
Lysianas'sa: a Nereïd. T258.

Machai, the: the Quarrels, children of Discord. T228.
Maia: daughter of Atlas. T938.
Maian'dros: a River. T339.
Manslaughters, the (Androktasiai): children of Discord.
    T228. In singular, S155.
Medei'a: daughter of Aietes and Idyia. T962; 993.
Medei'os: son of Jason and Medeia. T1001.
Medu'sa: a Gorgon. T276.
Me'lite: a Nereïd. T247.
Melo'bosis: an Okeanid. T354.
Melpo'mene: one of the Muses. T77.
Memnon: son of Tithonos and Eos. T984.
Menes'tho: an Okeanid. T367.
Menip'pe: a Nereïd. T260.
Menoi'tios: son of Iapetos and Klymene. T510.
Metis: an Okeanid. T358; 886; 929a.
Mimas: a Centaur. S186.
Mnemo'syne (Memory): daughter of Ouranos and Gaia,
    mother of the Muses. T53; 135; 915.
Mockery (Momos): son of Night. T214.
Moirai, the: the Destinies (or Fates), daughters of Night.
    T217.
Momos: Mockery, son of Night. T214.
Mopsos: a Lapith. S181.
Moros: End (of life), son of Night. T211.
Murders, the (Phonoi): children of Discord. T228.
Muses, the (Mousai): daughters of Mnemosyne and Zeus.
    T25; 77; 915; W1; 658.

Nausi'noös: son of Odysseus and Kalypso. T1018.
Nausi'thoös: son of Odysseus and Kalypso. T1018.
Nei'kea, the: the Grievances, children of Discord. T229.
Neilos: the Nile, a River. T338.

Nemeian Lion, the: child of Orthos and Echidna. T327.

Nemer'tes: a Nereïd. T262.

Ne'mesis: Decency, daughter of Night. T223. As public conscience, w197.

Ne'reïds, the: daughters of Nereus and Doris the Okeanid. T242.

Ne'reus: son of Pontos. T233; 240.

Nesai'e: a Nereïd. T249.

Neso: a Nereïd. T261.

Nessos: a River. T341.

Night (Nyx): child of Chaos. T107; 123; 211; 744; 748.

Nike: Victory, daughter of Pallas and Styx. T384.

Notos: the (south) Wind, son of Astraios and Eos. T380; 870.

Nymphs, the: children of Gaia. T130.

Nymphs of the Ash Trees, the: born of the blood of Ouranos. T187.

Oath (Horkos): son of Discord. T231; w219; 804.

Obri'areos: see Briareos.

Odys'seus: husband of Circe and Kalypso. T1012.

Oi'dipous: king of Thebes. w163.

Oizys: Pain, son of Night. T214.

Oke'anids, the: daughters of Okeanos and Tethys. T346.

Oke'anos: the Ocean Stream, son of Ouranos and Gaia. T133; 337.

Oky'pete: a Harpy. T267.

Oky'roë: an Okeanid. T360.

Old Age (Geras): child of Night. T225.

Onei'roi, the: the Dreams, children of Night. T212.

Onrush (Proïoxis): a Spirit. s154.

Orthos: dog of Geryon, son of Typhaön and Echidna. T293; 309; 326.

Oura'nia: one of the Muses. T78.

Oura'nia: an Okeanid. T350.

Ou'ranos: the Sky, son of Gaia. T106; 127; 155; 617.

Ou'rea: the Hills, children of Gaia. T129.

Ourei'os: a Centaur. s186.

Pains, the (Algea): children of Discord. T227.

Palio′xis: Backrush, a Spirit. s154.

Pallas: son of Krios and Eurybia. T376; 383.

Pallas: extra name of Athene. s126.

Pando′ra: the woman made by the gods. T571 (not named); w81.

Panic (Phobos): son of Ares and Aphrodite. T934; s144; 155; 463.

Panopei′a: a Nereïd. T250.

Parthe′nios: a River. T344.

Pasi′thea: a Nereïd. T246.

Pasi′thoë: an Okeanid. T352.

Peacetime or Peace (Eirene): one of the Seasons. T902; w228.

Pe′gasos: the horse born of Medusa's blood. T281.

Peiri′thoös: a Lapith. s179.

Peitho: an Okeanid. T349.

Pe′leus: husband of Thetis. T1006.

Pe′lias: taskmaster of Jason. T995.

Pemphre′do: one of the Graiai. T273.

Penei′os: a River. T343.

Perime′des: a Centaur. s187.

Perse′is: an Okeanid. T356; 957.

Perse′phone: daughter of Zeus and Demeter. T912.

Perses: son of Krios and Eurybia. T377; 410.

Perses: Hesiod's brother. w10; 274; 637.

Per′seus: son of Zeus and Danaë. T280; s216.

Petrai′e: an Okeanid. T356.

Petrai′os: a Centaur. s185.

Peu′keus: a Centaur. s187.

Pha′ethon: son of Kephalos and Eos. T987.

Phale′ros: a Lapith. s180.

Phasis: a River. T340.

Pheme: Gossip, a Concept raised to the status of Spirit. w760.

Pherou′sa: a Nereïd. T248.

Phi′lotes: Affection (or Friendship), child of Night. T224.

Phi′lyra: mother of Cheiron. T1001.

Phobos: Panic, son of Ares and Aphrodite. T934; S144; 155; 463.

Phoibe: daughter of Ouranos and Gaia. T136; 404.

Phokos: son of Aiakos and Psamathe. T1004.

Phonoi, the: the Murders, children of Discord. T228.

Phorkys: son of Pontos. T237; 270; 333.

Plei'ades: stars, daughters of Atlas. W383.

Plexau'ra: an Okeanid. T353.

Ploto: a Nereïd. T243.

Plouto: an Okeanid. T355.

Ploutos: son of Iasion and Demeter. T970.

Polydo'ra: an Okeanid. T354.

Polydo'ros: son of Kadmos and Harmonia. T978.

Polym'nia: one of the Muses. T78.

Ponos: Hardship, son of Discord. T226.

Pontoporei'a: a Nereïd. T256.

Pontos: the Sea, son of Gaia. T107; 132; 233.

Posei'don: son of Kronos and Rheia. T456; 930; W667; S104.

Pouly'noë: a Nereïd. T258.

Power (Kratos): child of Pallas and Styx. T385.

Proïo'xis: Onrush, a Spirit. S154.

Pro'lochos: a Lapith. S180.

Prome'theus: son of Iapetos and Klymene. T510; 521; W50.

Pro'noë: a Nereïd. T261.

Proto: a Nereïd. T248.

Protomedei'a: a Nereïd. T249.

Prymno: an Okeanid. T350.

Psa'mathe: a Nereïd. T260; 1005.

Quarrels, the (Machai): children of Discord. T228.

Respect (Aidos): a Spirit. W197.

Rheia: daughter of Ouranos and Gaia. T135; 403.

Rhesos: a River. T340.

Rhodei'a: an Okeanid. T351.

Rho'dios: a River. T341.

Rivalry (Zelos): son of Pallas and Styx. т384.

Rivers, the: sons of Okeanos and Tethys. т347.

Ruin (Ate): daughter of Discord. т230.

Sanga'rios: a River. т344.

Saö: a Nereïd. т243.

Seasons, the (Horai): daughters of Zeus and Themis. т901.

Sei'rios: either the star so named or the Sun. w417; 587; s153.

Sele'ne: the Moon, daughter of Hyperion and Theia. т371.

Se'mele: daughter of Kadmos and Harmonia. т940; 976.

Shame (Aidos): a Spirit. w317.

Si'moeis: a River. т342.

Skaman'dros: a River. т345.

Sleep (Hypnos): son of Night. т212; 759.

Speio: a Nereïd. т245.

Sphinx: daughter of Orthos and Echidna. т327; s33.

Starvation (Limos): son of Discord. т227; w299.

Ste'ropes: one of the Kyklopes. т140.

Sthenno: a Gorgon. т276.

Stories, the (Logoi): children of Discord. т229.

Strife (Eris): see Discord, Eris.

Strymon: a River. т389.

Styx: greatest of the Okeanids. т361; 383; 775.

Tar'taros: the pit beneath the earth, an original God. т119; 736; 821.

Tele'gonos: son of Odysseus and Circe. т1014.

Teles'to: an Okeanid. т358.

Terpsi'chore: one of the Muses. т78.

Terror (Deimos): son of Ares and Aphrodite. т934; s463.

Tethys: daughter of Ouranos and Gaia. т136; 337.

Thalei'a: one of the Muses. т77.

Tha'lia: one of the Graces. т909.

Tha'natos: Death, son of Night. т212; 759.

Thaumas: son of Pontos. т237; 265.

Theia: daughter of Ouranos and Gaia. T135; 371.
Themis: daughter of Ouranos and Gaia. T135; 901.
Themis'to: a Nereïd. T261.
Themisto'noë: daughter of Keÿx, wife of Kyknos. s356.
The'seus: son of Aigeus, ally of the Lapithai. s182.
Thetis: a Nereïd. T244; 1006.
Thoë: a Nereïd. T245.
Thoë: an Okeanid. T354.
Titans, the: the children of Ouranos and Gaia. T208; 716.
Titho'nos: husband of Eos. T984.
Tritogenei'a: by-name of Athene. T895.
Triton: son of Poseidon and Amphitrite. T931.
Tyche: an Okeanid. T360.
Typha'ön: husband of Echidna. T306.
Typho'eus: son of Tartaros and Gaia. T822.

Victory (Nike): daughter of Pallas and Styx. T384.
Violence (Hybris): a Spirit. w217.

Winds, the: children of Typhoeus. T869.

Xanthe: an Okeanid. T356.

Zelos: Rivalry, son of Pallas and Styx. T384.
Ze'phyros: the (west) Wind, son of Astraios and Eos.
    T379; 870.
Zeus: son of Kronos and Rheia. T54; 457; 883; 886; 901–
    929; 938; w2; 105; 169; 267; 465; s27; 383.
Zeuxo: an Okeanid. T352.

Ann Arbor Paperbacks

Waddell, *The Desert Fathers*
Erasmus, *The Praise of Folly*
Donne, *Devotions*
Malthus, *Population: The First Essay*
Berdyaev, *The Origin of Russian Communism*
Einhard, *The Life of Charlemagne*
Edwards, *The Nature of True Virtue*
Gilson, *Héloïse and Abélard*
Aristotle, *Metaphysics*
Kant, *Education*
Boulding, *The Image*
Duckett, *The Gateway to the Middle Ages* (3 vols.): *Italy; France and Britain; Monasticism*
Bowditch and Ramsland, *Voices of the Industrial Revolution*
Luxemburg, *The Russian Revolution* and *Leninism or Marxism?*
Rexroth, *Poems from the Greek Anthology*
Zoshchenko, *Scenes from the Bathhouse*
Thrupp, *The Merchant Class of Medieval London*
Procopius, *Secret History*
Adcock, *Roman Political Ideas and Practice*
Swanson, *The Birth of the Gods*
Xenophon, *The March Up Country*
Buchanan and Tullock, *The Calculus of Consent*
Hobson, *Imperialism*
Kinietz, *The Indians of the Western Great Lakes 1615–1760*
Bromage, *Writing for Business*
Lurie, *Mountain Wolf Woman, Sister of Crashing Thunder*
Leonard, *Baroque Times in Old Mexico*
Meier, *Negro Thought in America, 1880–1915*
Burke, *The Philosophy of Edmund Burke*
Michelet, *Joan of Arc*
Conze, *Buddhist Thought in India*
Arberry, *Aspects of Islamic Civilization*
Chesnutt, *The Wife of His Youth and Other Stories*
Gross, *Sound and Form in Modern Poetry*
Zola, *The Masterpiece*
Chesnutt, *The Marrow of Tradition*
Aristophanes, *Four Comedies*
Aristophanes, *Three Comedies*
Chesnutt, *The Conjure Woman*
Duckett, *Carolingian Portraits*
Rapoport and Chammah, *Prisoner's Dilemma*
Aristotle, *Poetics*

Peattie, *The View from the Barrio*
Duckett, *Death and Life in the Tenth Century*
Langford, *Galileo, Science and the Church*
McNaughton, *The Taoist Vision*
Milio, *9226 Kercheval*
Breton, *Manifestoes of Surrealism*
Scholz, *Carolingian Chronicles*
Wik, *Henry Ford and Grass-roots America*
Sahlins and Service, *Evolution and Culture*
Wickham, *Early Medieval Italy*
Waddell, *The Wandering Scholars*
Mannoni, *Prospero and Caliban*
Aron, *Democracy and Totalitarianism*
Shy, *A People Numerous and Armed*
Taylor, *Roman Voting Assemblies*
Hesiod, *The Works and Days; Theogony; The Shield of Herakles*
Raverat, *Period Piece*
Lamming, *In the Castle of My Skin*
Fisher, *The Conjure-Man Dies*
Strayer, *The Albigensian Crusades*
Lamming, *The Pleasures of Exile*
Lamming, *Natives of My Person*
Glaspell, *Lifted Masks and Other Works*
Grand, *The Heavenly Twins*
Allen, *Wolves of Minong*
Fisher, *The Walls of Jericho*
Lamming, *The Emigrants*
Loudon, *The Mummy!*
Kemble and Butler Leigh, *Principles and Privilege*
Thomas, *Out of Time*
Flanagan, *You Alone Are Dancing*
Kotre and Hall, *Seasons of Life*
Shen, *Almost a Revolution*
Meckel, *Save the Babies*
Laver and Schofield, *Multiparty Government*
Rutt, *The Bamboo Grove*
Endelman, *The Jews of Georgian England, 1714–1830*
Lamming, *Season of Adventure*
Radin, *Crashing Thunder*
Mirel, *The Rise and Fall of an Urban School System*
Brainard, *When the Rainbow Goddess Wept*
Brook, *Documents on the Rape of Nanking*
Mendel, *Vision and Violence*
Hymes, *Reinventing Anthropology*
Mulroy, *Early Greek Lyric Poetry*
Siegel, *The Rope of God*
Buss, *La Partera*